Remarkable Scientists

Stephen Hawking and Alan Turing

2 Biographies in 1

Michael Woodford and Anna Revell

Table of Contents

Stephen Hawking:

A Stephen Hawking Biography

The Greatest Scientist of Our Time

Michael Woodford

A brief history of Stephen Hawking

Dennis William Sciama (1926 – 1999) was a don at the University of Cambridge in the United Kingdom. He was one of the most eminent physicists of his time.

In 1963 he was informed that he was to receive a new pupil, a young man from Oxford who wished to undertake his doctoral thesis under his tutelage.

There was nothing unusual in this. Mentoring new pupils was part and parcel of a university academic's life.

However the new pupil seemed, on the face of it, unremarkable. In fact he had the reputation of a lazy and somewhat difficult student.

In his written exam at Oxford he had achieved neither a first nor a second degree. A first would have entitled him to undertake postgraduate studies at Cambridge; a second at Oxford.

He had to submit to an oral exam, an ordeal that terrified him but nevertheless impressed his examiners who remarked that they faced intelligence greater than there on.

After a while Sciama also agreed that he was dealing with a highly potent intellect.

This man was only 21 years old and moreover had just been given 2 years to live.

His name was Stephen William Hawking.

Hawking was born on January 8 1942 in Oxford, to Frank and Isobel (nee Walker) Hawking. He has two younger sisters, Phillipa and Mary, and an adopted brother, Edward.

Both parents were academics at Oxford University when Stephen was born. Frank read medicine while Isobel read philosophy politics and economics.

Frank would become head of the parasitology department at the National Medical Institute, London, in 1950.

But at the time of Stephen's birth the family was not prosperous. Frank's grandfather had bankrupted the Hawkings by incautious purchases during the Great Depression. It was only his wife that had saved them from utter disaster by opening a school in their home.

Isobel was the son of a Glasgow doctor who was determined to send her daughter to university at a time when an academic career (or a career of any kind beyond being in service, nursing or teaching) was considered highly unusual for women.

Oxford University did not even award degrees to women until 1920.

Perhaps it was this scape with ruin that made Frank Hawking a highly meticulous and methodical young man.

Isobel was more adventurous and hated being hemmed in.

When she was in confinement at hospital with Stephen (she was in her final week) she left the hospital and amused herself window shopping in the Oxford streets.

She went into a bookstore and there bought an astronomical atlas. Reflecting on the career her son would take, she regarded this as a propitious purchase.

The Hawkings were a bookish and somewhat eccentric family. Often meals would be spent in entire silence while Dad. Mom and Stephen read at table.

The family travelled in an old London cab, kept bees in the basement and made fireworks in the glasshouse. And Frank's specialty, tropical diseases, must have made for fascinating discussions over dinner, when they weren't all reading, of course.

Frank wanted Stephen to follow him into medicine, but Stephen had other ideas.

The boy loved science, and was often observed looking up on a starry night, lost in wonder.

Stephen was a very active lad. He was sociable, and loved to climb, play games and to dance.

As a student he was bright, though considered unexceptional. It may be that he considered the curriculum unchallenging, or else he did not have a strong enough focus for his mind. The latter would seem to be borne out by his university experiences.

The family moved to St Albans, a small city lying just to the north of London, when Stephen was eight.

He attended St Albans School. This all boys' institution is now fee paying, and is one of the oldest independent schools in the United Kingdom.

At the time of Stephen's education, however, it was a direct grant school. This meant that a number of students were awarded places on the basis of successful scholarship applications, whilst for others, normal fees were paid.

St Albans during the 1950s was a mixed bag of a school. It sported the astonishingly inappropriate motto 'Mediocria firma' – which translates as 'the middle way is safest'.

The motto was taken from the bi-sexual Elizabethan philosopher Francis Bacon, and caused Stephen's headmaster – WT Marsh – agonies of internal contradiction.

The man was duty bound the exhort, the traditions of the dictum whilst being horrified by association of the words with mediocrity – the last characteristic with which a school such as St Albans would wish to be associated.

(In fact, the adage related to the risky Elizabethan times, when to stray from the center ground could be seen as politically threatening, and would as like as not land the protagonist in serious, life threatening, danger.)

St Albans School in the 1950s was a somewhat eccentric place. A mixture of Masters and (occasionally) Mistresses taught the boys.

These teachers were intellectually extremely able, and may well have inspired the young Stephen onto future academic brilliance, but also bizarre in their behavior.

The cane was wielded widely, and not only by adults. Prefects were perfectly at liberty to beat boys who crossed boundaries – or not, in many cases.

In fact, an air of violence simmered beneath the surface of the old institution. WT Marsh would routinely lash out at students who annoyed him – a left wing sixth form poet often bearing the brunt of his anger.

He once used the death in a cycling accident of an old boy of the school as an opportunity for a brief lesson in the proper meaning of tragedy.

He described the young man's death as sad for his parents, but not tragic. That must have been a great comfort to them!

As a boy at St Albans, the young Stephen was given to what today we might consider creative but slightly offbeat behavior.

Whilst organized sports – as important to schools such as St Albans today as they were in the 1950s – held little appeal, he would create complex board games involving fantasy battles.

A kind of forerunner to Dungeons and Dragons.

In a harsh environment, only the strongest survive. St Albans was such a place, as were many fee charging schools of the time.

Those who opted out of the military aspect of schooling – it was possible to do so, but difficult – were routinely humiliated. They were given the task of building a Greek Ampitheatre at one point.

The task involving not only physically very challenging work (remember, they were still quite young boys) but to be carried out dressed just in shorts and t shirt – whatever the weather.

And although every single boy had passed a tough entrance examination to gain entry to the school – even those not in receipt of direct funding – to be cast in the bottom stream was considered academic failure.

Stephen was certainly not in this category. He sat comfortably half way through the A sets. If this seems surprising for a man who would become known as a genius, it is perhaps not that surprising.

St Albans and the surrounding region had seen a mass influx of European and Jewish immigrants during and after World War Two. Many of these families had trained their sons to achieve success at a school such as St Albans.

They possessed perhaps a work ethic and tolerance of the system that Stephen did not. The young Hawking also had a very eccentric mind, creative beyond the limits of the curriculum.

Whilst he certainly engaged with many of the very intellectual teachers, the curriculum of the time would offer little inspiration to him, being geared almost exclusively to winning an Oxbridge scholarship.

He was also a boy who liked to challenge the systems at St Albans. When older, he organized ban the bomb marches to Aldermaston, where the UK's chemical and biological warfare weapons are now developed.

Whilst Stephen did undertake the officer cadet training at the school, he did so with a kind of charming defiance, for example by refusing to keep his uniform smart.

And when on the firing range, long term hearing issues were far from the teachers' minds – it was seen as a weakness to require ear plugs.

However, quite happy to be regarded thus, Stephen created his own pair from blotting paper, which he stuffed so far down his ears that they had to be removed by the doctor the following day.

He as a small boy, and as such was a natural target for the bullying that prevailed at the school.

It seems as though he took it well enough, relying on his quick wit to put down the bigger boys, and accepting that sometimes he would escape, sometimes not.

In this simmering cauldron of a school, where explosions were always just around the corner, Stephen drew inspiration from his math master, Dick Tahta.

With the Armenian teacher, he built an early computer from discarded electronics.

And it is hard to argue against the ambience of the school leading Stephen on his journey to becoming the genius that lives today.

Although, it might have been his desire to be different from the norm that offered the greatest inspiration.

His parents were keen to give him an education as they had had, and he enrolled in the University of Oxford in1959, when he was only 17.

Oxford University is the oldest university in the English speaking, dating back to at least 1096 but probably much older than that.

The university was so prestigious and important in the life of the United Kingdom that until 1950 it elected two members to the British House of Commons.

The University has 38 colleges, to which in the Oxford and Cambridge Universities students must be affiliated.

Hawking joined the oldest of the Oxford colleges, University College. That college produced such men and women as the British Prime Minister Clement Atlee, US President Bill Clinton, the poet Percy Bysshe Shelley and the violinist Sophie Solomon.

Hawking enjoyed university life. He especially enjoyed the social life, as of course many university students do. He joined a rowing team as a coxswain. It was said that he was a somewhat enthusiastic, if not reckless, coxswain, losing oars and getting the team into dangerous scrapes.

And as is the case for many university students his studies tended to take second place.

He was bright and he knew it. He could write essays and take exams with a minimum effort and often with little, if any preparation.

While this got him through university he suffered from lack of application. His professors and tutors would comment on his lack of focus and carelessness.

It was only in his final year, 1963 that he realized he needed to focus on his energies and make up his mind what he wanted to do with an Oxford education.

In his final exam Hawking gained neither a First (qualification to undertake postgraduate studies at Oxford) nor a Second (to Cambridge). This necessitated an oral examination which Hawking regarded with trepidation.

Nevertheless he applied himself to the task and managed to achieve a Second. This was what he earnestly desired. He wanted to study for his doctorate under the tutelage of the great Cambridge physicist and cosmologist, Fred Hoyle.

But he was to be greeted by disappointment.

Reaching For the Stars

Sir Fred Hoyle (1915 – 2001) was a Cambridge University don and one of the foremost, if not the eminent astronomer of his day.

At a time when cosmology, the study of the origins and evolution of the universe, was in its infancy Hoyle was propelling it forward.

The idea that the universe was millions of years old and developed by physical laws and not by the direct intervention of a deity was still comparatively new.

In 1897 the famous physicist Lord Kelvin had proposed that Earth itself was probably around 20 million years old. We now know that estimate is ludicrously short, not nearly long enough to account for the formation of the world and evolution of life. Today scientists believe that close to 4 billion years is a more accurate estimation.

But how old was the universe itself?

Hoyle went part way to calculate an age by his work on stellar nucleosynthesis, that is, the formation and evolution of stars.

He showed that stars were formed by the coalescence of gas clouds under gravity. These dense clouds produced a colossal nuclear reaction that formed a star.

Moreover, as these stars run out of fuel they expand into such entities as red giants, and then collapse into smaller stars with colossal gravitational pull, such as white dwarves.

This evolution demonstrated that the universe had to be many billions of years old. Our Sun, for example, formed about 4 and a half billon years ago and is expected to last enough 10 billion years.

But stellar nucleosynthesis does not in itself tell us how old the universe itself is, nor does it answer an obvious accompanying question – did the universe have an origin and if so, how did it come into being?

This is of course the question that has absorbed humanity from its very inception. For centuries it belonged to the realms of religion and philosophy.

With the advent of science as we understand it in 16th and 17th century Europe were able to begin to answer how the universe functioned but still not how it came into being – if at all.

Its existence was still attributed to some supernatural creative principle, whether it was a personal God or an impersonal one who created and sustained the universe but without taking any interest in it.

In 1917 Albert Einstein proposed that the universe was static and essentially unchanging, implying that it had no origin.

Later he changed his mind after the famous astronomer Edwin Hubble (1889 – 1953), after whom of course the space telescope is named, observed that apparent clouds of gas in space called nebulae were actually galaxies, and appeared to be receding into space.

From this he deduced that objects in the observable universe were actually expanding away from each other.

Einstein adjusted his own theory in order to account for this, but still the apparent expansion could not be satisfactorily explained.

Enter Fred Hoyle. He agreed with Einstein that the universe was indeed essentially static and unchanging.

Stars were born and died, of course. But as a body is ordered and balanced by physical laws; the universe remained static. He called this model of the universe the Steady State Theory.

How then did Hoyle explain the apparent expansion of the universe? He supposed, without any definitive proof, that matter was continually being created in the spaces between galaxies.

So the universe was something like a pool of paint expanding because paint from a can is being continuously and evenly poured into it.

The Steady State Theory neatly avoids the problem of the origin of the universe by stating it never had one. The universe is eternal.

Apart from other scientific objections which are perhaps too complex to explore now, the theory does not answer the obvious question of how can something be produced from nothing?

This of course is a question that theologians are asked as well. And it was a question that was to be – and remains – the focus of Hawking's research.

Nevertheless Steady State Theory was widely accepted during the 50s and 60s, riding largely on the prestige of Hoyle.

Understandably Hawking was anxious to anxious to secure Hoyle's tutelage for his doctorate thesis.

However it was not to be.

Besides being a giant of astronomy and physics Hoyle was something of a scientific celebrity, much as Hawking would be.

He was constantly touring and giving lectures, being interviewed, writing, and using his status to intervene in fields often outside of his level of expertise.

For example, he famously entered the lists against paleontologists by in 1986 claiming that fossils of Archaeopteryx, a creature with affinities of both birds and reptiles and thus regarded as transitional between the two, were fake.

In the 1970s Hoyle proposed that life did not originate on Earth but instead evolved from microbes in meteors and comets that have struck Earth.

He curiously suggested that sudden and violent pandemics such as the 1918 Influenza Epidemic and the 1986 Mad Cow Disease outbreak in the United Kingdom were evidence of alien attacks.

Hoyle would have made an unsuitable tutor, being difficult to pin down and prone to going on tangents and fanciful ventures, none of which undermined his undoubted scientific prowess in the field of physics.

And there may have been another reason why Hoyle did not take young Hawking under his wing.

On one occasion Hawking was listening to Fred Hoyle lecturing at the Royal Society. At one point he interrupted Hoyle to correct him on something he saying.

Hoyle was astonished to hear someone who had barely graduated confidently daring to correct him, and must have been even more astonished to discover that Hawking was right.

So young Hawking got Denis Sciama.

Sciama had definite advantages over Hoyle that Hawking really needed at that time.

Sciama was brilliant, like Hoyle, but was not a celebrity. He was dependable.

Further he was genuinely solicitous for his students. He was encouraging and supportive, and recognized Hawking's unique intellect and also saw that it needed to be developed.

Hawking was in sore need of encouragement, for he had just been diagnosed with Amyotrophic lateral sclerosis (ALS), also known as Motor neuron disease or Lou Gehrig's disease.

This affliction is characterized by the normally rapid deterioration of muscle function leading to death.

The cause of the disease is unknown and there is no cure.

Hawking was already beginning to lose control of his body. He had falls and his speech was beginning to slur.

With his doctors giving him 2 years to live and faced with a horrible and humiliating decline, Hawking was depressed and in need of a reason to carry on.

He found comfort in his wife, Jane Wilde. The two had met at a News Years party at Cambridge. They became engaged in October 1964 and married on July 14 1965.

Hawking said that the marriage gave him 'something to live for', but before this Sciama encouraged the depressed young man to focus on his thesis.

Hawking chose as the topic for his thesis a theory of the origin of the universe – an ambitious task for a graduate!

He chose to contradict the mind that he had wanted as his tutor – Fred Hoyle. He did not wish to defend Steady State Theory. Rather he chose to advocate the other great theory of the origin of the universe – the Big Bang.

The father of the Big Bang theory was a Belgian priest, physicist and mathematician, Georges Lemaitres.

In 1927 Lemaitres explained the apparent expansion of the universe by positing that all matter had originally been condensed in a single point – a singularity.

This singularity then expanded, forming the universe which is still speeding outwards from the point when the singularity 'exploded'.

This idea came to be adopted by a number of physicists and astronomers who believed it best fitted the observable facts.

The theory had the advantage of not having to explain the creation of new matter, for all the matter that ever was contained in the primeval singularity.

However it could not explain what caused the initial expansion of the singularity. If all matter was contained in the singularity then what caused it to explode?

Further it did not explain where that matter comes from in the first place.

We casually and not entirely correctly use the word 'explode' but ironically Fred Hoyle used this terminology to condemn the idea.

In a 1949 radio interview he referred to the theory of a universe expanding outward from a single point as the 'Big Bang;' theory. And of course the name has stuck, the idea fiercest opponent actually giving the theory its name.

A major problem for the Big Bang theorists was proposing a mechanism. How could the entire mass of the universe be contained in a single point? There was no model, and no observable object in the universe that could provide a clue.

Nevertheless Albert Einstein had envisaged the possibility of singularities in his 1915 General Theory of Relativity.

In broad terms the General Theory of Relativity holds that there is no fixed object in the universe. Everything is in motion and is in motion relative to the motion of everything else. So a bird flying moves in relation to the movement of the air, which in turn is relative to the movement of the earth, the movement of the sun, of the solar system, the Milky Way, and so forth.

From this fairly straight forward observation Einstein extrapolated principles for time and matter.

For example, he concluded that as there was no fixed object, there was no fixed point of time either. Time was fluid.

From his General Theory of Relativity Einstein came up with a Special Theory of Relativity, which stated that energy and mass were mutually convertible. He composed the famous equation $E=MC^2$; an object is convertible to an amount of energy equivalent to the mass of that object multiplied by the speed of light squared.

We see an awful demonstration of this principle in nuclear fission, when an atomic bomb explodes, thought General and Special Relativity have a plethora of applications in the field of physics.

The young Hawking set his mind to applying these ideas to the concept of a singularity. His goal was grandiose. He wished to demonstrate that singularities could exist and in fact do exist, and that the origin of the entire universe from such a singularity could be satisfactorily explained.

In this he was inspired by the work of Roger Penrose (b. 1931), the English mathematician, physicist and science philosopher.

Penrose had written a paper postulating that the gravitational pull at the center of a black hole might be so insuperably strong that matter, space and even time itself was compressed into a singularity.

Now for us black holes are the commonplace stuff of science fiction films and novels, but when Hawking was writing his thesis they were little more than mathematical curiosities that had been postulated by the General Theory of Relativity.

Indeed the term 'black hole' was only adopted as a handy descriptive in 1964. At the time there was much theorizing about what the nature of a black hole would be.

Physicists can now tell us how bizarre black holes are, even though they are still shrouded in mystery and there is still much more they don't know about them than what they do know.

A black hole is a collapsed star, though not all stars become black holes. They arise from gigantic stars like red supergiant, which explode as a supernova and then gradually collapse into super-dense masses that exert so powerful a gravitational field that not even light can escape.

Strange things happen in black holes. The ordinary laws of space and time seem to disappear.

Einstein's General Theory of Relativity predicts that gravity curves matter. So if someone were to fall into a black hole they would appear to be stretched out like a piece of elastic.

Now gravity not only curves space, but time too. So something weird would happen to time too.

The closer an object moves toward a black hole the slower it travels in time. When that object reaches the event horizon, the boundary beyond which even light cannot escape, time would slow so much that it would appear to freeze – forever.

However, all this is what an observer would see. They would see, along with everything that was ever drawn by the black hole, a person stretched out and frozen in time.

On another level, the person would no longer exist for they would have been vaporized by the awful power of the black hole.

But suppose that person could survive, and plummeted into the depths of the black hole?

No-one knows. At the center of a black hole space and would be infinitely curved, becoming Penrose's singularity. The laws of the universe as we know them would no longer exist, and no-one knows what that would be like.

In his thesis Hawking proposed that the hypothetical singularity in a yet hypothetical black hole would provide the perfect model for the Big Bang.

Suppose that all the matter that is or ever was in the universe was compressed in a single point. Then that singularity exploded, releasing the matter and formed the universe.

For us the idea of the Big Bang is firmly embedded in the popular imagination, though we should remind ourselves that at the time the Big Bang was controversial, and the existence of black holes was not proven until one was discovered in 1971.

Hawking's thesis was therefore bold and inspiring.

It was so inspiring in fact that after obtaining his doctorate Hawking and Penrose decided to work further on the subject of singularities and the possibility of the universe originating from one.

In 1970 they together published a proof that the universe must have derived from a singularity.

Further theories came thick and fast. With physicists James Bardeen and Brandon Carter he composed a set of laws governing black holes.

Hawking described his research on black holes in his first book, entitled The Large Scale Structure of Space-Time, which he wrote with the mathematician and cosmologist George Ellis in 1973.

In 1974 Hawking accomplished what was perhaps his greatest achievement in the scientific field. In a paper he asserted that the proposition that nothing could escape the gravitational pull of a black hole is not entirely true.

According to Hawking, black holes emit radiation, very slowly and almost imperceptibly. After many eons the loss of energy causes them to shrink. As they shrink they become hotter.

Eventually they become so hot that they explode, and all the matter that has been subsumed into the black holes is released back into the universe.

At first this idea was controversial because it contradicted the widely accepted idea that a black hole was an absolute finality.

The theory of Hawking Radiation, as his idea is called, sees black holes not as the ultimate destroyers in the universe but as engines of creation. Black holes give rise to new stars and galaxies. They are, if you will, the great recyclers of the universe.

Hawking Radiation also answers a question about the universe's probable origin from a single point of singularity, much like a black hole.

If the singularity were a point of infinitely dense matter from which not only light could escape, how could the initial explosion possibly occur? What force could overcome the gravitational pull?

Hawking Radiation neatly avoids that problem by stating a black hole loses positively charged atomic particles at the event horizon, the point around a black hole beyond which the gravitational pull of a black hole is overpowering.

Negatively charged atomic particles continue into the black hole singularity.

The idea has become widely accepted, and it earned Hawking a Fellowship in the famous Royal Society of academics and scientists.

As yet there is unfortunately no direct proof of Hawking Radiation. That is why Hawking has not as yet been offered the Nobel Prize for this idea.

Following his hypothesis about Hawking Radiation Hawking speculated about a terrible possibility. He discussed the possibility that a collapsed black hole might very well wipe out the entire universe.

In a 1993 research paper Hawking supposed that sometimes a black hole that completely evaporates would leave a singularity. A singularity is a point of infinite density.

This singularity might be 'naked', meaning that the event horizon – the point beyond which not even light can escape – has disappeared also.

This means that the awful power of the singularity is exposed. There is nothing to stop the entire universe from being ripped apart by the rapidly spreading singularity

Now black holes take many billions of years to evaporate, and perhaps none ever has. On the other hand, perhaps a naked singularity is presently hurtling toward us.

Even so, it might take many millions of light years to reach us, so we can probably still book that holiday.

Hawking has said he prefers the speculative method in theoretical physics. He prefers to postulate an idea and see if the facts and the math fit his theory.

This means that occasionally he has been wrong, and on some quite important topics. But he has always been prepared to reassess the data at his disposal and admit his mistakes.

Hawking apparently has a penchant for making wagers with his colleagues over scientific questions.

For example, he bet a colleague, Kip Thorne, in 1975 that Cygnus X-1, a source of X-rays in the Cygnus constellation, was not in fact a black hole.

By 1990 it had become widely accepted, based on data that it was a black hole and Hawking conceded the bet.

Thorne's prize was a year's subscription to Penthouse magazine.

In 1975 Hawking was appointed Reader in Gravitational Physics at Cambridge University. By this time his speech was rapidly deteriorating, and he been using a wheelchair for several years.

He refused to concede anything to the disease that ravaged his body, and his family often remarked that he seemed to pretend that it did not exist, sometimes to their frustration.

He was notorious in the wheelchair, recklessly careering down the passages of Cambridge and occasionally running over feet.

After contracting life-threatening pneumonia in 1985 a tracheotomy was performed on him and he lost what remained of his speech.

This necessitated round-the-clock care and the employment of nurses working in three shifts.

It also meant that alternative methods of communication had to be devised.

At first cards were used, but in 1986 his famous voice synthesizer was devised and installed.

The synthesizer has an American accent because it was made in the United States. Hawking regards it as his own voice, and refuses to use any other. In fact, he has patented the voice so no-one else may use it.

At first he chose letters by moving a hand. However he has since lost movement in all but his cheeks and he uses his right cheek to manipulate the device.

From the many, many interviews we see recorded with Stephen Hawking, it appears as though his speech machine works much like a human voice.

Of course, when one considers the matter, this cannot be true.

In fact, speech is very slow, as he controls the machine with facial muscles to operate the sounds.

The impression we see during interviews comes about because Stephen has the questions in advance, and is able to 'pre-record' his answers to them.

Though his body declined his mind remained sharper than ever, and he seemed able to inhabit a world of pure intellect. Often he would spend hours by himself. Afterwards he would say 'I have solved that equation!'

However, he would soon be reminded of the limitations of his own body in a frightening and horrific manner.

Prisoner

In the 80s Stephen and Jane's marriage was breaking down.

Academically they were of different minds. Stephen thrived in the world of mathematical clarity and perfection. Jane enjoyed the comparative freedom and creativity of the humanities. She enjoyed music as well. Neither really understood the pleasures the others found in their disciplines.

Jane had a doctorate in Spanish poetry, and had felt compelled to obtain it in order that she might have an academic life at Cambridge distinct from that of her husband.

Jane was deeply religious. Stephen was, and remains, a firm atheist. At times he mocked her faith.

Jane found his devotion to the 'goddess Physics' ironic, given that it was she who made the decision to keep her husband on life support when he contracted pneumonia.

The doctors had given him up for dead, but Jane had faith that he could survive.

Jane formed a strong but platonic relationship with an organist from the church choir she belonged to. His name was Johnathan Hellyer Jones. Jae would later marry him.

This relationship was apparently accepted by Stephen.

Though devoted to her husband, Jane found attending to the needs of Stephen wearying, especially as he seemed oblivious to his condition and to the demands it made on others.

At length he did agree to hire extra help. University students took on the role of personal assistants and nurses undertook his physical care.

Though this did free Jane to pursue her own interests it also created a new pressure on their relationship.

Accompanied by aides for most of his waking hours Hawking was increasing isolated from his wife's influence.

As carers often do, Hawking's assistants developed a sense of responsibility that resented and excluded the influence of others, even that of his wife and children.

One carer in particular was assuming the position as the primary guardian of Hawking and interpreter of his needs.

This individual was Elaine Mason. She joined Hawking's nursing team in the 1980s. She rapidly assumed the first position in the caring team, excluding all but her own influence.

Hawking and Mason became close, and in 1995 he married her.

After their marriage Hawking's children and friends found themselves unable to approach him without going through Mason, who appeared to control every aspect of Hawking's life.

Then, in 2000, Hawking presented to a local hospital with a broken arm and a split lip. He refused to explain how he had come by them.

In January 2001, just shy of his 60th birthday, he presented again with a broken femur, saying that he had crashed into a wall.

To those who knew him this seemed odd, given that he was so adept in his wheelchair.

Many in Hawking's circle, including some of his nurses, suspected Mason. They spoke of hearing her scream abuse at her husband.

The police were called in by his daughter, Lucy, but Hawking refused to reveal how he sustained a string of injuries, decrying the intrusion into his private life.

On March 29 2004 Cambridge police dropped their investigation of Hawking's injuries, declaring it to be 'extremely thorough.'

However it was noted that only 12 people had been interviewed, and that Hawking himself vehemently denied the allegations that he had been physically abused.

'I firmly and wholeheartedly reject the allegations that I have been assaulted,' he said. In the light of these denials the investigators found themselves stymied.

Friends of Hawking were astonished. One concerned person had reported a conversation with him about Elaine. 'I cannot be left alone with her,' he said. 'Please don't go.'

Why then did Hawking refuse to admit to even his children that he was being assaulted? Given his attitude toward his debility, it may be that he did not want to draw attention to his vulnerability.

Perhaps the hold Elaine Hawking had over him was too strong, and he feared losing her. Relationships of dependency between the abused and their abusers are not uncommon.

On October 20 2006 Stephen and Elaine agreed to divorce. Hawking refused to comment on the divorce, regarding media interest and unwanted distraction, and to this day he has not spoken about the injuries he sustained during their marriage. There is no new investigation.

After their separation Hawking drew closer to his three children and indeed to Jane, who by now was married to Hellyer Jones. Jane always remained interested in and concerned for her ex-husband, and they remain close friends.

A Theory for Everything

Even during his personal trials Hawking remained focused on his academic pursuits. By his 60th birthday he had his mind set on the most ambitious intellectual goal of all – a theory of everything.

The Theory of Everything is the holy grail of theoretical physics. It is conceived as a sort of all-encompassing framework that would explain how everything in the universe works and fits together.

So far scientists have parts of an explanation. The General Theory of Relativity is one part. Quantum mechanics, the study of subatomic particles and their activity, is another. The four laws of thermodynamics governing energy are another.

The ultimate explanation, the glue that binds the myriad of physical laws together, is however missing.

Theoretical physicists aspire to come up with a mathematical equation that will answer everything. It would explain how the universe came into being. In particular it would explain where the initial matter in the came from. It would explain how something came from nothing!

To many, discovering this equation would be the pinnacle achievement of the human race. Scientific knowledge would be complete.

Others are anxious about the quest. They say that attaining such knowledge would be like eating the fruit from the Tree of the Knowledge of Good and Evil in the biblical Garden of Eden. We would become like gods, but terrible and immature in the way we exercise divine power.

For Hawking however there is nothing to fear. The quest for the Theory of Everything is for him the destiny of the human mind, which on Earth is privileged to reflect upon the wonders of creation and ponder their purpose.

He declared that a theory of everything, or Grand Unified Theory, as it is also called, was on the horizon in 1980s. He said that it had a good chance of becoming a reality by the beginning of the 21st century.

The publication of A Brief History of Time in 1988 marked Hawking's first venture into the realms of popular science.

He was approached by Cambridge University Press to write a book for laypeople about the universe and its evolution, using simplified terms and explanations.

Hawking was at first reluctant but he needed the money. He was initially frustrated by the editors, who insisted he keep simplifying his language.

The book popularized the work of Hawking, who until now had been a little known scientist beyond the halls of academia.

Hawking rapidly rose in the estimation of his peers and in 1979 he was appointed Professor to the Lucasian Chair of Mathematics at Cambridge.

This august seat of learning was founded by one Reverend Henry Lucas in 1663, and has been occupied by such intellectual giants as Isaac Newton and the nineteenth century inventor of the computer, Charles Babbage.

Hawking's research style is, by his own admission, more intuitive and speculative than evidence – based.

In other words, he makes informed speculations that seem to fit existing data and looks for the evidence to confirm the idea, rather than draw strict mathematical conclusions from the existing data.

'I would rather be right than rigorous,' he has said. For a scientist this may seem a rather casual way to seek truth. Hawking however sees this as creative. Many of his colleagues have been inspired by his ideas and scour the sky in search of evidence.

He has always been quick to acknowledge when the evidence has proved him wrong.

One instance of Hawking running into controversy with this method concerned a problem called the black hole information paradox.

All matter in the universe has information. By information scientists mean the mathematically quantifiable qualities that matter possesses – size, mass, width, temperature, and so forth.

When matter reaches the event horizon of a black hole it is vaporized, as we have seen. Yet the information of the matter remains.

We will remember when we were discussing black holes. The closer an object, say a spacecraft, approaches the event horizon the slower time becomes. So when it strikes the horizon an observer would still see the spacecraft forever, even though it is actually destroyed.

In other words, the information quantifying that matter would remain.

It's a tough concept to get the mind around. Even scientists have difficulty explaining it. But it makes sense mathematically given Einstein's theories of relativity.

However Hawking proposed in his theory of Hawking Radiation that a black hole very gradually evaporates, and that eventually it will disappear entirely.

But if that happened, where does the information of the spacecraft go? Does it disappear as well?

This was a problem for physicists, because it is a well-founded dogma of physics that information cannot be destroyed.

Hawking acknowledge the paradox and came up with a solution. He suggested that the information contained in matter falling into a black hole was preserved and released back into the universe by the outgoing Hawking Radiation.

However, this is a hunch on Hawking's part. It is unproven, just as Hawking Radiation itself remains unproven. Mathematically it is satisfying idea for many physicists. Yet there remains no concrete evidence to confirm the idea.

Hawking also courted controversy with the physicist Peter Higgs, over the latter's postulation of a universal field which gives everything in the universe mass.

Hawking strongly disputed the existence of such a field, until a particle of the field, the Higgs boson, was discovered by the powerful Hadron collider in Switzerland in 2013.

The so-called 'God particle' gives being to everything I the universe. Peter Higgs was awarded the Nobel Prize for predicting the existence of the Higgs boson and Higgs field in 2013.

Stephen Hawking was absolutely convinced that such a particle could not exist, and even bet with a colleague, Gordon Kane, that it would never be discovered.

Even after it was discovered he lamented its existence, complaining that it made physics less interesting.

He even suggested that the Higgs particle could mean the literal doom of the universe. While admitting the existence of the Higgs Field he suggested that it might at some point become unstable ad vaporize the universe.

While this may sound like sour grapes on Hawking's part, he has actually never been so petty as to deny evidence-based discoveries by his colleagues, even if Peter Higgs was awarded the Nobel Prize.

The discovery of the Higgs Field does however highlight Hawking's academic style and explain why he has never received the Nobel Prize himself, and perhaps never will attain that honor.

Hawking's research is highly creative. He prefers to speculate. Nobel Prizes are only given for proven scientific discoveries. Hawking Radiation, Hawking's greatest hypothesis, though widely accepted by scientists, remains an albeit highly informed mathematical speculation. No evidence has ever been discovered to confirm or deny its existence.

Hawking's creative mind impels him to make contributions beyond his field of theoretical physics. This is ironic, given that the scientists who could not be his postgraduate mentor, Fred Hoyle, proved unsuitable precisely because he too ventured into other realms.

Like Hawking, Hoyle was often before a camera presenting science to the public.

Hawking has warned humanity about creating an artificial intelligence that could be self-aware. Such an entity, he says, would assume an existence separated from humanity, evolve by itself and possibly enslave or destroy humanity in a horrendous Matrix or Terminator scenario.

He speaks about climate change and overpopulation and the diminution of Earth's resources.

He believes that Earth' resources could be consumed within around 100 years and then the human species will face extinction.

His solution is to colonize another world, and so he encourages the exploration of other solar systems and the development of technologies to transport humans to habitable planets in them.

The idea is not so outlandish as it may seem at first. Recent astronomical observations have indicated the existence of planets orbiting nearby stars. Some of these planets are similar to Earth in that they are not too close to their sun and not too far away as to make life impossible.

Hawking is a keen supporter of the Breakthrough Initiatives, a series of programs founded ad funded by the Russian entrepreneur Yuri Milner I 2015 to seek out habitable worlds and develop the technology to colonize them.

The Initiatives also hope to discover extraterrestrial life, and Hawking seems less keen on this venture.

Hawking's attitude to the possible of life on other worlds is cool and logical. He remains a skeptic about the existence of a deity. He believes the universe does not need one, and that eventually the human mind will be able to explain everything.

So for Hawking life is the result of a series of chance happenings, though no less wonderful for that.

Life on Earth then is statistically highly improbable. Life on other worlds must then be even more improbable still, and it remains possible that we are alone in the universe.

But if there are other intelligent life forms in the universe Hawking is not too keen to meet them.

If they are like us, he argues, and more technologically advanced than us, they have likely used up the resources on their own planet and have started to use the resources of others.

If they were to discover our world, they would most likely wish to colonize it, in much the same way that Europeans colonized the New World.

For Hawking intelligent life, whether it be biological or an artificial intelligence, is parasitical, controlling resources and fighting for control of them.

He does not approve of such behavior. He simple acknowledges it as an inevitably.

This nevertheless presents a rather pessimistic view of the concept of civilization, though it would seem to be borne out by facts.

Pessimistic though his views about humanity are it is probably fair to comment that he is encouraging people to talk about the problems that face our planet.

Back in the world of theoretical physics, Hawking's views were shifting. In 2010 he and Leonard Mlodinow published The Grand Design, a book covering the evolution of modern physics and cosmology.

In this book Hawking abandons his idea of finding a single explanation of the universe.

Instead he claims that there are five explanations.

His ideas are based on the supposition of minute, unobservable subatomic particles called strings. These strings vibrate in different modulations and each modulation represents a different state of being. And so the same string could have a number of alternate and simultaneous realities.

Each string theory has 11 dimensions, meaning that there are multiple alternate realities in the universe, each as true as the other, and consequently multiple explanations of reality.

This extraordinary and almost incomprehensible idea has been called M-Theory. The name is enigmatic, and the M has been interpreted as standing for 'magic' or 'mystery.'

However, like all Hawking's great ideas, it remains an informed hunch. It excites physicists, many of whom are striving to confirm it and solve some of the problems it presents.

From these ideas Hawking extrapolated one about the origin of the universe. It is useless, he postulated, to attempt to determine the origin of the universe, because it had a multitude of different origins.

This is based on the strange science of quantum mechanics, the workings of particles smaller than atoms. There the laws of physics as we know them in the macro world do not apply. There is a whole new set of laws that physicists are still only beginning to discover.

In the mysterious world of quantum particles different realities can co-exist. Indeed, this new field of research is exploding old ideas about the nature of space and time.

It has been suggested that time itself is not linear, flowing from the past through the present and into the future like a stream. Rather it may be the past and future occurs side by side in alternate but co-existing realities.

Time travel is another popular subject on which Hawking has been happy to speak.

He says that travel into the future is certainly possible. Indeed, it happens all the time.

The General Theory of Relativity holds that the closer an object approaches the speed of light the more it moves into the future relative to its starting point. In other words, time for that object s slows down.

So if a rocket or spaceship could be powered by a drive that would approximate the speed of light (according to the principles of relativity an object cannot supersede the speed of light) it could theoretically project an occupant forward in time.

Yet there would be a problem, in that the faster the craft went, the more mass it would take on .If a craft were theoretically able to fly at just short of the speed of light it would be so massive that the universe could scarcely contain it.

What of travelling in the past? According to the Einstein's General Law of Relativity, time can only travel forwards, not backwards.

However, there may theoretically be a way to travel through time. Hawking and other theoretical physicists speculate that a black hole could create a wormhole.

A wormhole would be a link between two points in space-time. But scientists have no idea how you would use such a portal. Firstly you would have to somehow avoid being crushed by the colossal power of a black hole.

Secondly, there is no way to predict what would happen, nor how a wormhole could be engineered to transport a person or object to a given point in space and time.

And even supposing it was possible to harness the power of a black hole to travel back in time would we want to?

Travelling backwards in time could create paradoxes. Suppose a person goes back in time and inadvertently kills his or own father before he was born?

If he kills his father he cannot exist. How then could he have gone back in time and killed him?

Hawking does not like that possibility. It disturbs the idea of an ordered, logical universe, and he has invented a law to stop it happening.

Tongue in cheek, he has proposed that quantum particles would instantly incinerate a time machine to prevent such a paradox being created.

But in typical fashion he presents a simple fact to dismiss the idea of travel into the past. If it is possible to travel backwards in time, where are the time travelers? Where are the tourists who have come to visit the past?

Perhaps they have come, and we have had them sectioned. Or perhaps they are in disguise, under strict instructions not to interfere in history.

Hawking conducted an experiment to determine once and for all whether time travel into the past was possible.

He held a party for time travelers. He posted the open invitation on YouTube. It read 'You are cordially invited to a reception for time travelers hosted by Stephen Hawking to be held at the University of Cambridge.'

He included geographical co-ordinates and the date, adding 'no RSVP required.'

However, he did not post the invitation until after the date.

He prepared a room with balloons, champagne and nibbles and waited.

Alas, no-one turned up.

World's Greatest Living Genius?

In the popular imagination Stephen Hawking is perhaps the greatest living mind. Indeed one would be hard-pressed to think of any other scientist who has captured the attention of the world as much as Stephen Hawking.

There is the physicist Brian Cox, well-known as a presenter and writer of popular science. However his own contribution to physics is relatively small.

Likewise if we move beyond physics and consider biology, we can consider Richard

Dawkins, known primarily not for science at all but for his criticism of religion.

In contrast Hawking stands out not only for his popular explanations of science via television and the printed word but for the substance of his ideas.

His grandest idea concerns the fundamental and universal question every human being has asked – how did the universe come into being?

Hawking explained to the world, through his work on black holes, how the entire cosmos was flung out of a singularity.

We might ask ourselves however, as critics have, how the science expounded by

Hawking has been conflated with celebrity appeal. Is it possible to critique his ideas without critiquing the personality behind those ideas?

Critics remind us that his greatest ideas, inspiring though they may be and framed by brilliant calculations, are largely intuitive hypotheses, yet unproven.

Hawking Radiation remains unproven, and scientists have pointed out huge problems even in his idea of the Big Bang.

First there is the problem of where the matter dormant in the singularity came from. Hawking hopes to demonstrate sometime in the future how something can come from nothing, but for now it remains a difficulty.

Some researchers point out that the Big Bang seems to violate the Law of Entropy, which says that matter becomes less organized over time. Yet if this is so how do the stars and galaxies seem to be so incredibly complex and organized?

There are, after all, scientific alternatives to the Big Bang theory. Some scientists postulate a Big Bounce rather than a Big Bang. In this model our universe is one of an infinite series of contracting and expanding universes, neatly avoiding the problem of creation from nothing.

There are other theories as well. And yet the Big Bang remains the first, and for many the only, known theory of the universe. Few persons apart from physicists seem able to fully grasp the concept, and yet it has gripped the world.

Are we listening to the man rather than the idea? Has Hawking become some sort of demagogue, the high priest of science?

We are reminded too that Hawking has been wrong on a number of occasions and has freely admitted this.

And then we should consider the elephant in the room. Stephen Hawking is a man who lives in his own mind. His brain is the prisoner of a body that no longer obeys it. Or to put it another way, his mind has been freed from the distractions of the body and the demands of the flesh.

So has Hawking become for us a sort of scientific saint? Is he a mental ascetic, transported by the denial of the flesh to some higher plane we mere mortals can only dream of?

Doubtless Hawking himself would balk at the suggestion, but perhaps we are projecting our own conceptions of genius and disability upon him, and unfairly so.

Hawking has never wanted to be seen as disabled, but perhaps the perception of genius in him enables us to frame him within our own flawed, romanticized ideas of what disability means.

Perhaps unconsciously we are influenced by the romantic idea of the savant, the individual limited in one aspect, yet gifted by nature in another by way of compensation.

Hawking would certainly not thank us for this back-handed compliment, nor agree with the logic of that idea. He does not believe there is justice inherent in the universe. There is only the inevitable flow of course and effect, without intent or purpose.

Hawking rarely talks about himself, and almost never speaks about his feelings. However he did speak on the relationship between his illness and his work.

'When you are faced with the possibility of early death,' he said, 'it makes you realize life's worth living, and there are lots of things you want to do.'

He is not trying to beat death, but rather to live each day as fully as he can, which is great advice for anyone.

He says he does not play to the media, nor use it to spruce his ideas. The purpose of his media appearances and books (he even wrote a series for children with his daughter Lucy) is simply to explain his work to the public, something he considers important.

He admits that his research won't affect the daily lives of people very much at all. Black holes, string theory and quantum mechanics won't cure diseases or end famine or bring world peace, 'but it is important to understand where we come from and what we can expect to find as we explore.'

It does not appear that Hawking is a theoretical physicist for the fame and glory. He does what he does because he loves it.

So could it be that he does not want to share his genius with the world? He doesn't want to prove anything. He's just a guy using his talents and having a great time doing it.

The Theory of Everything and Other Media Portrayals

In 2014, two films were released in the United Kingdom which, at first glance, appeared unlikely to make any kind of impact on the cinema going public.

The reason for this was their subject matter – in both cases, they focused on the lives of true British Heroes.

But very much not of the James Bond kind. No, the subject of these films was intellectual geniuses who had made their mark on the culture and history of the country.

That the lead actors in these films were two of the bright young sparks of English acting added to the appeal.

And that they had attended well known, competing public schools further raised the anticipation.

The comparisons between Eddie Redmayne playing Stephen Hawking in 'The Theory of Everything' and Benedict Cumberbatch's portrayal of Alan Turing in 'The Imitation Game' became the talked about thing in British cinema.

Redmayne is an old Etonian. Whilst there, he had once played the back end of an Elephant in a house play.

By contrast, Cumberbatch is an old Harrovian. The two schools are competitors. Geographically they are quite close – Harrow being in North London, Eton just to the West of Heathrow.

They compete over their alumni. Eton might throw former Prime Minister David Cameron but Harrow can trump with Winston Churchill (although, apparently, he hated the school).

Eton counters with the Royal Princes, Harrow check mates with…Winston Churchill.

Turing, the subject of Benedict Cumberbatch's film, was the mathematical genius who solved the enigma code.

This was the machine Germans used during the Second World War to send out messages to its navy operators, and from which they would launch attacks on convoys crossing the Atlantic.

Turing worked at Bletchley Park, a converted manor house in the center of England from where code breakers operated during the war.

He created the machine which was able to interpret the German Enigma codes, solve them and, many would argue, lead the allies to victory in the war.

'The Imitation Game' is a great film, but it was trumped by the unlikely success of a film about a disabled scientist.

Eddie Redmayne described the challenges of playing Stephen Hawking, for which he won an Oscar.

Firstly, his burgeoning admiration for the man presented its own problems. He had spent six months researching into Hawking, and became gradually to see the scientist as an idol.

So when they met for the first time, he spewed a nervous barrage of conversation at his subject, his anxiety and delight at meeting his new hero combining to make him virtually unintelligible.

During the research phase, Redmayne was extremely thorough.

He visited victims of amyotrophic lateral sclerosis (motor-neurone disease). In fact, he spent four months at the National Hospital for Neurology and Neurosurgery's clinic learning about the condition.

He talked to Stephen's family. He read (without full comprehension) 'A Brief History of Time'. He watched footage of his subject.

The film was to be about Hawking's university days, when he both met his wife and inspiration, Jane Wilde, and when he contracted the life destroying medical condition.

He had wanted to be as prepared as possible before meeting the great man, but now

Redmayne was about to be introduced to the person he would be playing, he began to have doubts.

What if the research he had undertaken had given him a false impression of the scientist?

But, once he had calmed himself, Redmayne learned much from the meeting.

He discovered that Stephen's voice had become extremely slurry during the onset of his disease.

The presented a problem that he and the director, James Marsh, had not really considered. They were left with a conundrum.

On the one hand, they wished to represent Hawking and his condition in as honest a light as possible, but equally they did have to produce something their audience could understand.

It is all very well being true to the story, but if the audience cannot understand it, then that story is not being told.

Subtitles were a possibility discussed. But both director and actor felt that these would detract from, rather than clarify, the tale they wished to tell.

The resulting speech added much to the power of the story.

Another thing that Eddie Redmayne had not fully grasped was the humor and vitality of the scientist.

Although physically he is able to use only a very small number of muscles, the cheeky, energetic and offbeat humor of the eleven year old starting out at St Albans School back in the 1950s is still present.

It was the addition of this that enabled the story to be a powerful tug on the emotions, rather than a maudlin tale.

Redmayne worked with a dance teacher to train his body to be able to adopt the uncomfortable positions into which Stephen's body has contorted.

It was important to do this first. After all, Redmayne would also be portraying a character in love, and it was important that the physical factors did not detract from his concentration on this.

He learned that one thing suffers from the condition do is to concentrate as much into their few remaining active muscles as possible.

These become conduits for expressing their emotions, and showing themselves.

With Stephen Hawking, it was his face, and especially his eyebrows, that continued to show the real man.

Redmayne worked hard, studying footage extensively, to try to capture how these normally insignificant facial features worked.

However, 'The Theory of Everything' is not the only occasion in which Stephen Hawking has appeared on film.

Not by a long chalk.

It is a part of his appeal that he is so media friendly. After all, most of us would probably struggle to name any other living scientists, but Stephen's name would be first on the lips during any quiz.

Perhaps one of his most famous roles has been in TV's hit cartoon comedy, 'The Simpsons'.

Stephen's daughter, Lucy, knows one of the scriptwriters on the US show, and learned that they wanted to write an episode featuring the scientist.

She persuaded her father to take part. He voiced himself to his cartoon presence a number of times.

He appeared in the season 10 episode, 'They Saved Lisa's Brain', which was also used in archive footage in a season 11 episode.

He also took part in several more performances. These include the season 16 episode 'Don't Fear the Roofer'; season 18's 'Stop or My Dog Will Shoot!' and the season 22 show 'Elementary School Musical'.

Stephen also appeared in a documentary special – 'The Simpsons: A Culture Show'.

Given the longevity of the show, and the desire of world renowned figures from popular culture to be involved, it is another remarkable achievement that Stephen appears in the top 20 of IGN's 'Top 25 Simpsons Guest Stars'.

He rolls in at number 16 – quite remarkable for a cosmologist.

Stephen wrote the 2010 mini-series 'Into the Universe with Stephen Hawking'. This series was created for the discovery channel. It aired both in the US and in Britain.

However, in Britain, it was known as 'Stephen Hawking's Universe.'

With a neat touch of irony, voice overs were recorded by the actor Benedict Cumberbatch, who would of course be the lead in the rival film to Eddie Redmayne's 'The Theory of Everything' in a few years' time.

In the science series, Hawking appears in person in each of the episodes – 'Aliens', 'Time Trael' and 'The Story of Everything'.

In the last of these, some footage was used for an episode of another documentary, 'Curiosity'.

'Star Trek' is, as we all know, one of the great science fiction series of all time, and in this Stephen Hawking created a 'first'.

In the episode 'Descent, Part 1' – the denouement of Season Six of 'Star Trek: The Next Generation' he appears as a hologram.

He is shown playing poker with two other fairly recognizable names from the world of science, Sir Isaac Newton and Albert Einstein.

However, the notable point about this is that he played the hologram himself. In doing so he became the first ever guest on 'Star Trek' to play himself.

Just as with 'The Simpsons', and the ironic portrayal of card playing on 'Star Trek', comedy is one of Stephen's favorite genres for film and TV.

Not surprising, perhaps, given his generally funny demeanour.

He appeared in the British TV comedy legend 'Red Dwarf'. Stephen is a fan of the series, and has praised the writers for their witty use of faux-science.

He has also taken part in the huge US science based comedy show 'The Big Bang Theory', which stars Jim Parsons.

He has appeared in no fewer than six episodes, often as a voice over. The episodes are:

'The Hawking Excitation', The Extract Obliteration', 'The Relationship Diremption', 'The Troll Manifestation', 'The Celebration Experimentation' and 'The Geology Elevation'.

Most years in the United Kingdom, a large charity event is held called Red Nose Day.

Created by comedian Lenny Henry as a way to tackle poverty in Africa, the charity is now a part of British Culture.

It features various zany events taking place around the country, and stars appear on the live show, where people pledge money.

Often in return for those stars doing something funny, but undignified. Each year, a new design of Red Nose is created, plus versions for your car.

With enormous self-irony, Hawking appeared in 2015 in which he 'transforms' into a 'Transformer'.

The sketch featured two cutting edge British comedians alongside Hawking – Catherine Tate and David Walliams.

He also took part in a sketch with Jim Carrey on 'Late Night with Conan O'Brien'. The left field, slightly seditious 'TV Offal' featured him in the title sequence.

Other appearances on TV include presenting the trophy for the winners of the tough quiz show, University Challenge.

He has been involved in numerous science based documentaries including 'Genius of Britain', where he was link man for a series on famous British Scientists.

He was a participant in the documentary 'The 11th Hour' and 'Alien Planet'. He also hosted, through voice over, a science fiction series 'Masters of Science Fiction.'

Hawking's first connection with the actor Benedict Cumberbatch happened during the filming of the TV Movie 'Hawking'.

With surprising similarity to the major Hollywood film some years later, this film too portrayed Stephen's time Cambridge.

Cumberbatch played the eponymous lead in the film.

Stephen was also portrayed by an actor in an episode of 'Stargate Atlantis'. 'Brain Storm' and as well in 'Superhero Movie.'

On top of his various appearances in 'The Simpsons', he is also a regular in 'Futurama', having been a character in the following episodes.

In 'Anthology of Interest' he appears as a guard of the space-time continuum. 'The Beast with a Billion Backs' he has a somewhat curtailed role as he is shown as simply a head in a jar.

'Family Guy' is another cartoon show which has drawn heavily on Hawking. He has appeared in seven episodes, most recently as a streaker in a basketball game.

He is a video game character in the episode entitled 'reincarnation'.

Such is his recognizable voice, and so well and warmly is he regarded, that he is often subject to gentle parody, particularly in British comedy shows.

A character from the hit series 'The Vicar of Dibley', Frank (whose character is renowned for being boring) chooses to portray his role as a Wise Man in a Nativity play as having Hawking's voice.

Keeping with the faux-religious theme, he is referenced in the comedy 'Father Ted.'

Other times he has been referred to in a similar way include the American hit 'Seinfeld' amongst many others.

He has appeared widely in commercials; include some for the high end marque Jaguar.

Stephen also pre-recorded an amusing skit featuring his wheel chair for a Monty Python show.

In fact, his media appearances and representations are myriad. Amongst the enormous number not listed here is the use of his voice on a Pink Floyd album.

Perhaps one of his favorite lampoonings involved the satirical news publication 'The Onion'.

In it the periodical runs an article claiming that Hawking has designed a high powered robotic exoskeleton.

In keeping with his love of a joke, Stephen wrote a letter published in the paper in which he claims that they have unveiled his plans for world domination.

It is remarkable, and of enormous merit, that a man so physically afflicted could encounter life with such positivity and sense of fun.

Hawking is also a prolific writer. Some of his works have been discussed already in this book, but in fact he has produced no fewer than twenty-six publications for which he is either co or sole writer.

This is in addition to the far too many to mention articles he has written.

As a closing point for this biography, we will look at a collection of eight of these books which might well slip under the net.

Co-written with his daughter Lucy, Stephen has produced this mini collection written specifically for children.

The 'George' series feature George and his best friend Annie. The intrepid duo travel into space, learning (as is the case with their readers as well) about scientific principles as they go.

The stories capture the off-beat, funny and creative side of Stephen which we saw right back from a young child, when he would abandon Monopoly for games of his own, complex, making.

An example of the creativity in the George books can be taken from their 2014 publication 'George and the Unbreakable Code'.

In this wonderful story, we see the libertarian, anti-establishment Hawking shine through. Banks hand out free money, supermarkets stop being able to charge for food and aircraft refuse to fly.

All because super computers appear to have been hacked.

In another of their books, 'George and the Big Bang', he demonstrates the respect for young people that will always win their adoration.

He explores one of his most complex theories despite the youth of his audience.

Here, George is having a few domestic problems and even his best friend Anne seems to have other things on her mind.

So, he sets out to help another mate, Eric, develop his plans to go back to the beginning of the universe.

The story features evil doing villains and takes the form of a story, collection of essays and even a graphic novel element.

'George's Secret Key to the Universe' explores physics, science and the universe as a whole through a thrilling series of adventures.

In this story, a super computer with its own intelligence (called Cosmos) takes Annie, her father Eric and, of course, George on an exciting trip to the edge of a black hole – and hopefully home again.

The theory of black holes explained through comedy and adventure.

Brilliant.

Stephen Hawking is not just a genius. He is an educator and a man with a razor sharp wit and enormous sense of fun.

In his own words

My advice to other disabled people would be, concentrate on things your disability doesn't prevent you doing well, and don't regret the things it interferes with. Don't be disabled in spirit as well as physically.

No one undertakes research in physics with the intention of winning a prize. It is the joy of discovering something no one knew before.

Science is beautiful when it makes simple explanations of phenomena or connections between different observations. Examples include the double helix in biology and the fundamental equations of physics.

While physics and mathematics may tell us how the universe began, they are not much use in predicting human behavior because there are far too many equations to solve. I'm no better than anyone else at understanding what makes people tick, particularly women.

I regard the brain as a computer which will stop working when its components fail. There is no heaven or afterlife for broken down computers; that is a fairy story for people afraid of the dark.

I was never top of the class at school, but my classmates must have seen potential in me, because my nickname was 'Einstein.'

It is generally recognized that women are better than men at languages, personal relations and multi-tasking, but less good at map-reading and spatial awareness. It is therefore not unreasonable to suppose that women might be less good at mathematics and physics.

A few years ago, the city council of Monza, Italy, barred pet owners from keeping goldfish in curved bowls... saying that it is cruel to keep a fish in a bowl with curved sides because, gazing out, the fish would have a distorted view of reality. But how do we know we have the true, undistorted picture of reality?

Obviously, because of my disability, I need assistance. But I have always tried to overcome the limitations of my condition and lead as full a life as possible. I have travelled the world, from the Antarctic to zero gravity.

God may exist, but science can explain the universe without the need for a creator.

In less than a hundred years, we have found a new way to think of ourselves. From sitting at the center of the universe, we now find ourselves orbiting an average-sized sun, which is just one of millions of stars in our own Milky Way galaxy. Stephen Hawking

The human race may be the only intelligent beings in the galaxy.

I think computer viruses should count as life. I think it says something about human nature that the only form of life we have created so far is purely destructive. We've created life in our own image.

If the rate of expansion one second after the Big Bang had been smaller by even one part in a hundred thousand million, it would have re-collapsed before it reached its present size. On the other hand, if it had been greater by a part in a million, the universe would have expanded too rapidly for stars and planets to form.

I don't have much positive to say about motor neuron disease, but it taught me not to pity myself because others were worse off, and to get on with what I still could do. I'm happier now than before I developed the condition.

We are just an advanced breed of monkeys on a minor planet of a very average star. But we can understand the Universe. That makes us something very special.

The usual approach of science of constructing a mathematical model cannot answer the questions of why there should be a universe for the model to describe. Why does the universe go to all the bother of existing?

God not only plays dice, He also sometimes throws the dice where they cannot be seen.

I believe everyone should have a broad picture of how the universe operates and our place in it. It is a basic human desire. And it also puts our worries in perspective. Stephen Hawking

Science is increasingly answering questions that used to be the province of religion.

It's time to commit to finding the answer, to search for life beyond Earth. Mankind has a deep need to explore, to learn, to know. We also happen to be sociable creatures. It is important for us to know if we are alone in the dark.

My discovery that black holes emit radiation raised serious problems of consistency with the rest of physics. I have now resolved these problems, but the answer turned out to be not what I expected.

I can't disguise myself with a wig and dark glasses - the wheelchair gives me away.

If we do discover a complete theory, it should be in time understandable in broad principle by everyone. Then we shall all, philosophers, scientists, and just ordinary people be able to take part in the discussion of why we and the universe exist.

I think the brain is essentially a computer and consciousness is like a computer program. It will cease to run when the computer is turned off. Theoretically, it could be re-created on a neural network, but that would be very difficult, as it would require all one's memories.

I'm not afraid of death, but I'm in no hurry to die. I have so much I want to do first.

The radiation left over from the Big Bang is the same as that in your microwave oven but very much less powerful. It would heat your pizza only to minus 271.3*C - not much good for defrosting the pizza, let alone cooking it. Stephen Hawking

I was not a good student. I did not spend much time at college; I was too busy enjoying myself.

So long as the universe had a beginning, we could suppose it had a creator. But if the universe is really completely self-contained, having no boundary or edge, it would have neither beginning nor end: it would simply be. What place, then, for a creator?

Before I lost my voice, it was slurred, so only those close to me could understand, but with the computer voice, I found I could give popular lectures. I enjoy communicating science. It is important that the public understands basic science, if they are not to leave vital decisions to others.

We must develop as quickly as possible technologies that make possible a direct connection between brain and computer, so that artificial brains contribute to human intelligence rather than opposing it.

Even if there is only one possible unified theory, it is just a set of rules and equations. What is it that breathes fire into the equations and makes a universe for them to describe?

Alan Turing: Enigma

The Incredible True Story of the
Man Who Cracked The Code

Anna Revell

Introduction

If you have ever used a computer, you owe that joy to Alan Turing. Turing is known by many as the Father of the Modern Computer for his conception of the theoretical stored-memory machine (known as the Turing Machine) and for the subsequent implementation of this idea in the creation of some of the world's first working computers, the Automatic Computing Engine, and the Manchester Mark 1.

Essentially, Turing not only conceived of the possible existence of a computer that could perform more than one task, he was also instrumental in helping several computer labs actually bring his ideas to life. He saw his concepts go from mere theory to actual reality in his lifetime. Everything he theorized was then built on by new generations of computer scientists, and eventually led to the technological wonderland in which we live, and often take for granted, today.

Impressive as they are, though, Turing's contributions to computer science are not necessarily his most famous or influential projects. Alan Turing was one of the most significant figures in the Allied victory of World War Two, thanks to his ingenious code breaking skills and the invention of the British Bombe at Bletchley Park. In his later life, Turing even dabbled in artificial intelligence, and biology, creating concepts that are still being investigated today.

Until recently, Alan Turing had often been overlooked as an important figure in history. Thanks to in-depth biographies like Andrew Hodges' Alan Turing: The Enigma, and film depictions of Turing's life, like The Imitation Game, based on Hodges' book, Alan Turing is quickly becoming a household name, as people begin to recognize that his contributions to various fields were so influential they actually changed the course of human history.

Early Life

Alan Mathison Turing was born on June 23rd, 1912 at Warrington Lodge, a nursing home in Paddington, England. The Turings, Ethel and Julius, were temporarily back in England at the time, while Julius took leave from his work in the Indian Civil Service in British India. Ethel wanted her children, Alan and his brother John, to be born and grow up, in England.

Alan was an absent-minded, stubborn, and precocious child. He paid little attention to what other people around him wanted. He often delayed his mother or nanny for long periods of time while they were out running errands just so he could carefully inspect small things like lamppost serial numbers.

As careless as he could be, he was also detail-oriented, curious, meticulous, and, when something grabbed his attention, singularly-focused.

His nanny later remarked on "his integrity and his intelligence for a child so young" after Alan got extremely upset when he noticed she had let him win at a game. It was remarkable that a child so young even noticed he was being fooled, and even more remarkable that he respected the game play so much.

Alan's independent nature didn't lend itself to traditional schooling. He wanted to study what he was interested in, when he wanted to study it, not what the school told him to learn, when they told him to learn it.

At age 10 Alan was sent to Hazelhurst, the preparatory school his brother John was attending at the time. John was a popular boy, and a good student. He even became head boy at the time Alan joined him at the school.

In 1922 Alan got his hands on a book that would change his life. Natural Wonders Every Child Should Know was an American science text for children. The book basically opened Alan's eyes to the existence of science as a study, and a legitimate pursuit. It also introduced the idea that God had less to do with natural phenomena than Alan had been taught his whole life. Alan devoured this book and took it with him wherever he went.

Unfortunately for Alan, science was not a focus in British schools at the time. He was pushed to study language, including Latin, and classics. His parents allegedly weren't displeased with his interest in science. They encouraged his passion, buying him a chemistry set for Christmas in 1924, and attempting to answer what questions they could.

Alan's mother has said that she recognized and encouraged his genius from the beginning. His brother, however, completely refutes this claim. He said, "The truth of the matter, as I now view it in retrospect, is that neither of Alan's parents or his brother had the faintest idea that this tiresome, eccentric and obstinate small boy was a budding genius". He claimed their mother was constantly "trying to press him into a conventional mould." After his death, Alan's journals would reveal that he severely disliked his mother, possibly because she was not as nurturing of his talents as she claimed to be.

Whether or not the Turings encouraged Alan's scientific genius is up for debate. What is certain is that they wanted Alan to get into a good public school. This would require Alan to pass the Common Entrance Exam, a test that focused on languages and classics rather than science or math.

Alan continued his interest in science, but also studied for the entrance exam. He took it once in 1925 and did fairly well; and again in 1926 after which he was accepted into Sherbrooke School in Dorset.

On his first day of Sherbrooke there was a general strike that halted trains and busses. With no way of getting to his new school, Alan opted to cycle the 60 miles from his home town to Dorset. This incredible feat foreshadowed Alan's impressive athletic ability, and was even written about in the paper. Later, when he worked at Bletchley Park, Alan would find a penchant for long distance running. He was often said to run to meetings in London that were over 40 miles from Bletchley Park, rather than take the train. He won many races in his athletic club, and was said to be a near-Olympic level marathoner.

Alan's odd personality made him fairly unpopular with his classmates. As he was still an unfocused, stubborn student, he didn't have any fans on the staff at Sherbrooke, either. His housemaster called him "undeniably...not a 'normal boy'".

Alan continued his interest in science and mathematics to the detriment of his other subjects. He was also uninterested in the other, more social aspects of the school in which the boys were pushed to participate. Sherbrooke was focused on moulding well-rounded citizens who were not only top students, but were social, athletic, and generally well-trained.

Nowell Smith, Sherbrooke's headmaster, wrote to the Turings and told them that

Alan's singular focus on science did not fit with the Sherbrooke philosophy. He wrote, "If he is to stay at a Public School, he must aim to be educated. If he is to be solely a Scientific Specialist, he is wasting his time at a Public School."

Though he began to take more of an interest in subjects other than science, and began to do better, Alan was still held back in fifth form. He was, however, allowed to take sixth form mathematics, as that was obviously his strong suit.

In 1927 Alan began looking closely at Einstein's work questioning Galilei-Newtonian axioms. He actually managed to continue Einstein's work, and properly explain the scientist's viewpoints on the axioms that his written work never made completely clear.

It was around this time that Alan met Christopher Morcom, a fellow science enthusiast, and the man generally believed to be Alan's first love. The two studied science and mathematics together, and worked on problems in their spare time.

Christopher was more of the exemplary Sherbrooke student; social, well-rounded, and a good student in all his subjects. His interest in Christopher inspired Alan to try a little harder at the subjects that didn't interest him as much as science. Soon he was allowed to properly join the sixth form, and was delighted to have all his classes with Christopher.

Since childhood Christopher had been struggling with complications from bovine tuberculosis that he had contracted from drinking infected cow's milk. His condition had been worsening during his time at Sherbrooke. Christopher Morcom died in February of 1930. Alan was devastated by the loss of his friend, and decided to throw himself further into his studies, as he believed that is what Christopher would have wanted from him.

In a letter to Christopher's mother Alan wrote, "I am sure I could not have found anywhere another companion so brilliant and yet so charming and unconceited. I regarded my interest in my work, and in such things as astronomy (to which he introduced me) as something to be shared with him and I think he felt a little the same about me ... I know I must put as much energy if not as much interest into my work as if he were alive, because that is what he would like me to do."

It may have been partly Christopher's death that set Alan on the path that would define his entire career. Not only did Alan throw himself into his studies as a tribute to Christopher, which led to many academic opportunities, he also began thinking about what makes up a human.

Alan was a firm atheist, but, due to his friend's death, he began grappling with the concept of the spirit, and its connection with the mind and body. He became almost fascinated with his own grief, wondering how Christopher still had such a presence in his life, even though he had died. How could a man's spirit have such a pull on him when the man had ceased to exist? What is the spirit if it is not something that is connected to the physical body, and may continue to linger in one's mind after the death of the body?

Alan wrote again to Christopher's mother on the topic of the spirit saying, "Then as regards the actual connection between spirit and body I consider that the body by reason of being a living body can 'attract' and hold on to a 'spirit' whilst the body is alive and awake and the two are firmly connected. When the body is asleep I cannot guess what happens but when the body dies the 'mechanism' of the body, holding the spirit, is gone and the spirit finds a new body sooner or later perhaps immediately."

It is particularly interesting that Alan essentially called the body a "mechanism" that holds onto the spirit. Many of Alan's future projects would involve him attempting to explain or create a mechanical brain; a thinking entity that existed outside a human body. It was almost as if Alan was trying to build his concept of a spirit.

The mechanical brain idea informed his most seminal work; the concept of the Turing Machine, the implementation of that concept in the form of a stored-memory computer, and the idea of a Turing Test for artificial intelligence. Had Alan not suffered such a loss, and not ruminated on the concept of the spirit, his career may have taken a different path altogether.

Further Study

Alan kept his personal promise to the late Christopher Morcom. He studied hard and was admitted to King's College at Cambridge University, where he studied Mathematics. Finally able to study what he wanted, Alan did exceptionally well. He was elected fellow of King's College in 1935 for his dissertation that proved the central limit theorem.

Alan also felt more personally free at Cambridge. It was a more liberal and accepting environment and Alan was able to freely have relationships with other men without fearing judgement or persecution.

Turing's most notable work at Cambridge was in his paper On Computable Numbers, with an Application to the Entscheidungsproblem.

In this 1939 paper, Alan developed the idea of a stored program computer. He called it a universal computing machine, but it is now more well-known as a Turing Machine. It was a theoretical machine that consisted of a scanner, and a line of unlimited tape. The tape would be divided into squares that were either blank, or had one symbol on them (usually a 1 or a 0).

The scanner would look at each square individually, read the instruction programmed on the square, and perform an operation based on the four functions it would be programmed to perform. Any given square on the tape could tell the machine to either move left one square, move right one square, print a symbol on the square, or change it's state, meaning move on to the next set of instructions.

The example Turing gave in his paper can be summed up in the following table:

State	Scanned Square	Operations	Next State
a	Blank	P[0], R	b
b	Blank	R	c

c	Blank	P[1], R	D
d	Blank	R	A

In this scenario the machine would start with state 'a'; if the square it scanned was blank it would print a 0 on it, then move right one square and move onto the instructions in state 'b'; if the next square was blank, it would simply move right and move on to state 'c'; if that square was blank it would print a 1 on it, and move right again, to state 'd'; if that square was blank it would move right and loop back around to the instructions in state 'a', where it would start again.

His paper had been an answer to David Hilbert's Entscheidungsproblem. American mathematician Alonzo Church had also been working on the same problem at Princeton University. Church came up with a completely different, though equally valid answer. He was so impressed with Turing's work that he invited him to Princeton to work under him as a doctoral student so they may further study the problem. In September 1936, Alan moved to America to study under Church. Their work on computable functions is known as the Church-Turing thesis.

In June 1938 Alan Turing received his PhD from Princeton University with his dissertation Systems of Logic Based on

Ordinals. In this paper Turing introduced the idea of ordinal logic.

He returned to England in 1938 and almost immediately began working for the Government Code and Cypher School. Britain declared war against the Axis powers on September 3rd, 1939. On September 4th, Alan reported to Bletchley Park to begin working on cracking the Enigma code.

The Enigma

Perhaps Alan Turing's most famous work had to do with breaking the German wartime code, known as the Enigma.

The Enigma machine was initially created by Arthur Scherbius after World War One in order to protect business secrets that were being sent across wires through Morse Code. The Enigma is a typewriter-like machine with two keypads, each housing all 26 letters. When the user presses a letter key on the bottom keypad, it generates an electric current which gets scrambled by the machine through a system of crossed wires. The machine then lights up a different letter on the top keypad. The newly generated letter then stands in for the actual letter in the code.

Unlike other letter substitution codes, though, Enigma would encode one single letter as a different letter every time that letter was pressed. There was not a simple substitution where every A in the code became a B, and every B became a C, etc. An A might become encoded as an L the first time you pressed it, and come out as a Z the next.

This feature made it harder to begin cracking the code, as cryptographers would often begin with a double letter (like the two Ls in "Hello") and work backwards from there, knowing that certain double letters are more common in certain languages than others.

You would also be unable to find out what one letter stood for, and substitute that letter for every encoded letter. You couldn't know that every time an A showed up in the code it was actually a Y, as the Enigma machine would encode every A as a different letter.

The Enigma code was made even more difficult to crack because of the machine's many parts and the number of variations possible for each part during the assembly of the machine. Initially each Enigma machine had three rotors with the entire alphabet on each of them. These could be placed into the machine in any order, with any one of the letters as the starting point. Each of the rotors had a ring attached to it which could be moved to one of four different positions. The machine also had a patch panel of letters on the front of it. Each one of these letters would be connected via cable to another letter, and would manipulate the path of the electrical current flowing through the machine.

There were thousands of potential combinations. It was the perfect machine for sending wartime messages, and it was soon co-opted by the Nazis to communicate in the various arenas of battle.

Even with such astronomical odds, the Germans still didn't want to risk anyone cracking their code. The way each Enigma machine was assembled changed at midnight. Of course this was before automation, so the configuration for each day was found in a code book or chart that accompanied the machine, and done by hand. The chart explained in what position the rings on the rotors should be, at which letter each rotor was to begin, the order in which the rotors were to be placed in the machine, and the letter pairings for the front patch panel.

As if all that security wasn't enough, the Germans also encoded a separate Enigma start position for each individual message. It was a three letter code that corresponded to the rotor settings, that was then, itself, encrypted with the daily Enigma setting. In a cryptographic error, the new three letter position was encoded twice. The operator would receive a correspondence that looked like 6 random letters, and decipher it into two sets of the same three letters. He would then set the machine up accordingly, and finally be able to decode the actual message the other operator was attempting to send.

Using intelligence gathered from both commercial Enigma machine research and from German informants, Polish mathematician Marian Rejewski worked out that, due to the three letter code being encrypted twice, there was necessarily a relationship in the wiring of the Enigma machine between the first and fourth letters, the second and fifth, and the third and sixth.

Cryptanalyst Henryk Zygalski figured out that in about 1 out of 8 messages, one of the plaintext letters encrypted to the same letter twice. For example, the first and fourth letters would be encrypted from the same letter into the same, albeit different, letter. Maybe an ABCABC would turn into a TVDTNS. The As both became Ts. These sets were called females. From this occasional relationship between letters, Zygalski created a method to narrow down possible Enigma settings.

Though Zyglaski's method was effective, it was also done by hand which made it slow and inefficient. Rejewski created a machine that automated the process. He named it the bomba kryptologiczna, or the cryptologic bomb. It was a device that deduced the wiring of the Enigma machine. Each bomba represented six Enigma machines, and did the work of 100 people attempting to break the code by hand.

There are several stories as to why the machine was dubbed bomba. Oddly, one story says it was named after the ice-cream treat of the same name, though that doesn't make much sense as the two have absolutely nothing to do with one another.

A more likely story was told in a U.S Army report in 1945. It stated, "A machine called the "bombe" is used to expedite the solution. The first machine was built by the Poles and was a hand operated multiple enigma machine. When a possible solution was reached a part would fall off the machine onto the floor with a loud noise. Hence the name 'bombe'". It was both loud and used to speed up a process, much like a bomb.

Rejewski, though, simply claims it was called bombe "for lack of a better idea".

The Germans eventually figured out their code was being cracked and, in 1939, made two major changes to avoid the security hacks. They added two more possible rotors (IV, and V) to the army and air force Enigma machines. This changed the possible number of rotor configurations from 6 to 60, and brought the possible combinations of the machine up to a whopping 158,962,555,217,826,360,000. For the all-important naval Enigma, the Germans added five more rotors, bringing the possible configuration of rotors up to 336, with the possible combinations of parts coming to over 180,000,000,000,000,000,000.

The Germans also stopped repeating the three letter starter code at the beginning of messages. These changes significantly affected the bomba's ability to break the Enigma code, as the Germans had now removed the clues the machine used to deduce the Enigma setup. The Poles then decided to share their equipment and knowledge with the British and French so that their allies may continue their work, and the Germans could be defeated.

The final blow to the Polish attempts at cracking Enigma came in 1939 when Germany invaded Poland. The cryptanalysis office opted to destroy their research, lest the Germans get their hands on a bomba, realize their code had been compromised, and completely change their communications tactics.

Bletchley Park

Meanwhile, at Bletchley Park in England, Alan Turing and his team were working on their own ways to crack the Enigma code.

Bletchley Park was an English code breaking camp around 50 miles from London. It was first dubbed Bletchley Park in 1877 when Samuel Lipscomb Seckham bought the site and the mansion that sat upon the grounds. In May 1938, Hugh Sinclair, the head of MI6, bought the site with his own money after the government branch claimed they did not have the budget to buy the property.

Sinclair liked the spot for the Government Codes and Ciphers School for several reasons. It was across the street from a multiline train station that would connect many important cities; it was far enough outside of London to avoid being damaged in any air raid that might take place in the event of a war; it was also more or less equidistant between Cambridge and Oxford Universities, two prestigious schools from which code breakers would be recruited.

MI6 initially operated out of the ground's mansion from when they moved in on August 15th 1939. In late 1939, though, prefabricated huts began to be erected, and the boarding school near Bletchley Park, Elmers School, was acquired and used as part of the operation.

Bletchley Park was known to have been populated with the brightest minds England could muster. Of course mathematicians, statisticians, and scientists were brought aboard, but MI6 did not stop with these traditional fields. They recruited bridge experts, linguists, chess champions, historians, and many others with specific and rare bases of knowledge.

The organization even had The Daily Telegraph set up a cryptic crossword competition to scout for potential employees. They asked whether anyone could finish the cryptic crossword in under 12 minutes. These people were then invited to the Telegraph office to sit another crossword test. This time they were told to complete the puzzle in under six minutes. The winners of the competition were discreetly approached and asked if they would like to be involved in "a particular type of work as a contribution to the war effort".

Everyone who worked at Bletchley Park had to sign the Official Secrets Act 1938, but the secrecy did not stop there. Employees were discouraged from even speaking to each other about their individual projects.

They were told, "Do not talk at meals. Do not talk in the transport. Do not talk travelling. Do not talk in the billet. Do not talk by your own fireside. Be careful even in your Hut."

In September 1934, four influential men were recruited to work at Bletchley Park by Commander Alastair Denniston. Aside from Alan Turing, MI6 also brought on Gordon

Welchman, Stuart Milner-Barry, and Hugh Alexander. They were some of the earliest recruits for the code breaking operations at Bletchley Park, and became known as The Wicked Uncles.

Gordon Welchman became the head of Hut 6, which worked cracking the German air force and army Enigma code. Irene Young, a worker in the Decoding Room of Hut 6 said, "Operators were constantly having nervous breakdowns on account of the pace of the work and the appalling noise." Indeed, codebreakers at Bletchley Park worked around the clock to try and get any lead on a potential solution.

Welchman, unable to fully decipher any Enigma message, set his sights on something else. He began simple traffic analysis of the messages the team was intercepting. Welchman paid close attention to callsigns of encrypted German messages, and to where these messages were coming from, and going to. Eventually this led to Welchman deducing the callsign for a large majority of German bases, ships, outposts, and, notably, weather stations. The team at Bletchley Park began to piece together a map of the entire communications system used by the Germans.

Turing was working as the head of Hut 8, attempting to crack the naval Enigma. He knew that certain greetings and indicators were used daily by German officers. For example, he knew that each morning a German U-boat would send out a weather report at the same time, using not only the German word for weather report (Wetterbericht), but the same order of information: wind speed, atmospheric pressure, temperature.

U-boats also often sent the message "Keine besonderen Ereignisse", or "no special occurrences." Using this information Turing was able to create what became known as cribs, basically the team's best guesses for what the Enigma layout for the day might be.

Laying an intercepted message overtop something like the German "Wetterbericht", which he knew would be going out at a certain time in the morning, Alan Turing was able to make a guess as to how the Enigma was set up for that day. Turing also noted one major flaw in the Enigma machine; it could not encrypt a letter as itself. No As became As in the encrypted code. This narrowed down thousands of possibilities for Enigma configuration. If you laid out a message and the W in "Wetterbericht" matched with another W in the encrypted code, you could be certain that was not the configuration of the Enigma machine. This was called crib dragging.

Using his knowledge of the Polish bomba, and the principles of elimination he deduced himself, known as Banburismus, Alan created the British Bombe. Like the Polish machine, the Bombe was a code breaking machine that basically ran through all the possible Enigma settings until it produced a readable, understandable plaintext, free from errors. When it had finished its job, the team would then have the Enigma configuration for the day and be able to decipher the rest of the messages that would be intercepted that day. The first British Bombe was installed in Hut 1 at Bletchley Park on March 18th, 1940.

The Bombe wasn't a magical code breaking machine. The Enigma code still had billions of possibilities for its configuration. The Bletchley team still needed cribs to kickstart the deciphering process.

As one such crib, Bletchley Park code breakers used what were known as kisses. A kiss was an identical message that was sent in two different codes, one of which had already been broken. It was called as kiss as the codebreakers designated one with an 'xx', the traditional short form for kisses in written correspondence sent to a loved one.

The German navy often used both the Enigma, and a dockyard cipher, a hand cipher which was much easier to break. Germans would send the same message out in both codes and, as Bletchley Park had most likely already broken the dockyard cipher, they could compare the two identical messages, and figure out the Enigma for the day.

Bletchley Park also acquired cribs through 'gardening'. This referred to the process of coaxing certain known words out of the Germans. The British would plant mines in certain places knowing that the Germans would send out warning messages with the locations of the mines, what area or harbor was nearby, and, probably the word 'mine'.

Again, the U-boats would send out these messages in both Enigma, and the simpler dockyard cipher. Being able to cross reference the same message in both the easier, broken cipher, and the more difficult Enigma, gave Bletchley Park valuable intel into what the Enigma setting was for the day.

Once the codebreakers collected these cribs they could then pass their best guesses through the Bombe, and the machine would run through the possibilities that remained.

At first the Bombe runs could take days. When Gordon Welchman modified Turing's initial bombe design with a diagonal board the machine was then able to cross check hundreds of possible solutions at the same time. This cut down the time it took to find the solution to the Enigma code from days to mere hours. After Welchman's modification, the codebreakers would generally have the Enigma solution for the day by the early morning, after starting at midnight when the new Enigma configurations were meant to be set.

Occasionally German officers didn't bother changing their Enigma settings from the previous day, giving Bletchley Park a huge advantage.

Turing was also able to develop the Eins Catalogue as a crib system. Bletchley Park knew, thanks to information gleaned from an interrogation of a German prisoner of war, that numbers in an Enigma cipher were always coded in complete, spelled out letters, not in abbreviations or substitutions. Turing took this information and, using backlogged broken codes, discovered that 'eins', the German word for 'one' was used in almost every message the Germans sent. It was by far the most used four letter word in their messages.

Once the rotor setting for the day had been determined there were still over 17,000 possible configurations for the word 'eins'. Alan catalogued each one of these possibilities in alphabetical order so that, if a certain string of four letters came up in a message, the codebreakers would have a possible shortcut for figuring out the rest of the code. They would pull the Enigma machine configuration from the catalogue once a possible 'eins' was found, test that configuration, and, if it produced coherent German they had cracked the code for the day.

British intelligence could not let on that they had broken the code, or that they were even attempting to do so. If the Germans realized the Allied had figured out the Enigma code they would change their communications systems, and Britain would be left in the dark with no possible way to glean new and necessary intelligence.

The Allies, therefore, had to decide which pieces of information they received were essential to winning the war, and which could be overlooked in the name of keeping their knowledge secret. Some German attacks were allowed to go on, even though the British knew they were imminent. They also sent dummy ships out to certain locations so the Germans could see the enemy vessel, and assume anything the Allies turned out to know about German locations or plans came from the ship they had seen days prior.

Unfortunately this strategy did lead to damaged ships, fewer supplies, and, most tragically, lost lives. However, many more lives were ultimately saved by letting the

Germans believe their code was, indeed, unbreakable.

Since the beginning of the war German U-boats in the North Atlantic had sunk over 700 Allied ships, destroying hundreds of tonnes of supplies, and taking several lives.

Winston Churchill, the wartime British Prime Minister was quoted as saying, "...the only thing that ever really frightened me during the war was the U-boat peril." If supplies could not be moved across the Atlantic then Britain may have just been essentially starved into submission. The North Atlantic was also important for bringing troops to Europe for D-Day operations.

The loss of the naval corridor would have been disastrous for the Allies. This tension was referred to as The Battle of the Atlantic. In cracking the Enigma, the code breakers salvaged supply lines, and saved valuable supplies, ships, and lives.

In late October, 1941, The Wicked Uncles (Turing, Welchman, Alexander, and Milner-Barry) co-signed a letter addressed to Churchill explaining what their operation had done toward winning The Battle of the Atlantic, and their need for more resources to continue their work.

The letter read, "Some weeks ago you paid us the honour of a visit, and we believe that you regard our work as important. You will have seen that, thanks largely to the energy and foresight of Commander Travis, we have been well supplied with the 'bombes' for the breaking of the German Enigma codes. We think, however, that you ought to know that this work is being held up, and in some cases is not being done at all, principally because we cannot get sufficient staff to deal with it. Our reason for writing to you direct is that for months we have done everything that we possibly can through the normal channels and that we despair of any early improvement without your intervention."

Churchill, so impressed with Bletchley Park's successes, and equally worried about losing the Atlantic supply lines immediately moved on the request. He wrote to General Ismay saying, "ACTION THIS DAY. Make sure they have all they want on extreme priority and report to me that this has been done."

By mid-November Bletchley Park had all the resources they needed to continue their essential work, though apparently the codebreakers were unaware of the Prime Minister's strong support. Milner-Barry later recalled, "All that we did notice was that almost from that day the rough ways began miraculously to be made smooth."

Alan had a brief engagement in 1941 to Joan Clarke, a fellow Hut 8 codebreaker. Clarke was mentee of Gordon Welchman at Cambridge University. He recruited her in 1940 to work at Bletchley Park. Their engagement only lasted a few months. Alan had admitted to Joan that he was gay. Joan said she was "unfazed" by the revelation and wanted to marry him anyway. Both recognized marriage as more of a social duty than an actual partnership based on romantic love. It was not necessarily commonplace at the time to marry for love, and it was quite unusual to remain single, so the arrangement worked for both parties.

Alan ultimately decided he did not want to go through with the marriage, wanting to give Joan the opportunity to be in a legitimate relationship. They dissolved their relationship, but remained close friends for the rest of Alan's life. In 1952 Joan married a colleague at her post-war job at the Government Communications Headquarters.

In February of 1942 the Nazis introduced a fourth rotor to their Enigma machine, this new configuration was codenamed Triton in Germany, and Shark in England. The extra rotor made it much more difficult to crack the code. Casualties in the North Atlantic again began to rise and Bletchley Park had to scramble to attempt to break the code of what appeared to be an entirely new machine.

Turing was sure there was to be some relationship between the old three rotor machines, and these new four rotor ones, as not all the Enigma machines across all German communication lines had been converted, yet the Germans continued to communicate with one another.

Eventually it was discovered that the fourth rotor was not a removable one, like the others, but a stationary one with only 26 possible settings. Had it been a new removable rotor, the naval Enigma rotor configurations would have increased from 336 to 3,024. It was certainly not as disastrous a change as it could have been, but still made the problem of the Enigma 26 times more difficult, and would; thus, require 26 Bombes for every one currently in operation.

The codebreakers did occasionally get some insight into this new rotor. The fourth rotor was usually set to a neutral position on U-boats. In December 1941 Bletchley Park intercepted a message that was unintelligible, followed by the same message in the proper code. Bletchley Park was able to deduce that the first message had come from the U-boat operator accidentally knocking the fourth rotor out of the neutral position, and encoding the incoherent message on a setting that did not make sense.

The subsequent message allowed the codebreakers to figure out the wiring of the fourth rotor. This was useful information, but did not mean the team could automatically increase their cracking speed back to where it was before the fourth rotor was introduced. Bombe runs still sometimes took days instead of hours.

MI6 did not only rely on broken Enigma code for their intelligence. Much of the codebreaking done at Bletchley Park also used the code books and lists retrieved from sunken U-boats. Unfortunately it was not until 9 months after the switch from the three rotor machine to the four rotor machine that Britain was able to get the new books. It was clear that Bletchley Park clearly needed help with intelligence gathering.

They had been keeping their methods top secret and, even with America's entrance into the war in December of 1941, still refused to share their code breaking methods with their allies. However, with the new four rotor machine slowing down their abilities, and losses in the Atlantic increasing daily, Bletchley Park decided to show the Americans how to build their own Bombe. Alan was sent to America in November-

December 1942 to aid the National Cash Register Corporation in creating a functional and secure Bombe.

Alan seemed amused at what the Americans assumed codebreaking at Bletchley Park was like. He said, "The American Bombe programme was to produce 336 Bombes, one for each wheel order. I used to smile inwardly at the conception of Bombe hut routine implied by this programme, but thought that no particular purpose would be served by pointing out that we would not really use them in that way."

Turing explained to the Americans that, using his elimination methods, they would not need 336 machines, only 96. By just a year later America had 120 Bombes. They became fast, efficient code breakers, and aided Britain greatly in cracking the German naval Enigma for the remainder of the war.

Alan returned to Bletchley Park in March 1943 as a general consultant for cryptanalysis.

The codebreakers at Bletchley Park are credited with hastening Nazi defeat by two years, and saving thousands of lives.

Post-War Career

On 1945, Turing was awarded the Order of the British Empire for his wartime service, though the circumstances surrounding the award were not disclosed, as his contributions to the war effort were still classified.

In 1945 Alan began working at the National Physical Laboratory. There he wrote Proposed Electronic Calculator wherein he detailed the circuitry, hardware, coding, and even cost expectation for the Automatic Computing Engine.

The ACE was a continuation of Turing's 1936 concept of a stored program computer that gave rise to the idea of the Turing Machine.

However, now that electronic advances had been made, and Turing himself was much more well versed in computing due to his experiences at Bletchley Park, the theoretical concept of a Turing Machine could, potentially, become a reality.

Machines at the time were essentially single use apparatuses. They were built to perform one function, and performing that function was the only thing they did. If you wanted a machine to perform a different function you would need to rewire it completely. Turing's computer would have programs installed into it that could perform different functions based on the instructions in the program.

Interestingly, Alan didn't seem to care that much that his concept of the ACE would revolutionize machinery, and basically invent modern computer science. He was more interested in creating machines that mimic the functioning of a human brain. He said, "In working on the ACE I am more interested in the possibility of producing models of the action of the brain than in the practical applications to computing."

In 1946 Turing and his team at the National Physical Laboratory worked on a program library for the ACE, even before the computer itself was built. The Laboratory did not have the funding to begin to build the physical computer. One story says that the NPL didn't believe Alan's proposed budget was sufficient, and that they were unsure some of his plans would work out. However, because he had gotten his information from his work at Bletchley Park, Alan could not disclose to the Laboratory how he knew his plans and figures were sound, so the project was delayed.

Alan became increasingly frustrated with the delay in manufacturing the ACE and, in 1947, he returned to Cambridge for a sabbatical year, with the expectation that he would come back to work at the NPL when he had completed his year of independent research.

That is not what ended up happening. Manchester University scouted Turing for a position in their computing lab. In 1948 he was appointed the position of Reader in the Mathematics Department at Manchester's Victoria University. Turing resigned from the NPL, breaking the implied terms of his sabbatical, and greatly infuriating his former colleagues at the National Physical Laboratory.

Turing was to work on Manchester's own stored program computer, the Manchester Mark 1. In April of 1949 the Mark 1 was operational and, in the same year, Turing became Deputy Director of the Computing Lab at Manchester University.

Turing continued to be fascinated by the idea of a computer as a mechanical human mind that possesses all the capabilities of the working human brain. Of the Manchester Mark 1 he said, "This is only a foretaste of what is to come, and only the shadow of what is going to be. We have to have some experience with the machine before we really know its capabilities. It may take years before we settle down to the new possibilities, but I do not see why it should not enter any of the fields normally covered by the human intellect and eventually compete on equal terms."

In 1950 the Pilot ACE was built without Turing's aid at the National Physical Laboratory. It ran its first program on May 10th, 1950 and was, for quite some time, the world's fastest computer. Though he was not present for the actual building of the machine, and his full vision of the ACE was not actually created until after his death, he is still credited as the genius behind the machine's invention.

In 1950 Alan wrote the paper Computing Machinery and Intelligence. It was an early foray into the concept of artificial intelligence, and a continuation of Alan's interest in building mechanical a "brain". In his paper he asked the question, "Are there imaginable digital computers which would do well in the imitation game?"

The Imitation Game was a party game where a man and a woman were separated from the rest of the guests, and from each other, and the crowd had to attempt to tell which person was which, based on their typewritten answers to several questions. However, each player was trying to convince the guessers that they were the other player.

Turing's test of artificial intelligence, aptly named the Turing Test, works in much the same way. The idea is that you have two humans, A and B, and one machine, that are all separated from each other. Human A must then ask Human B and the machine a series of typewritten questions. If Human A can't tell which answers are coming from Human B, and which are coming from the machine, the machine is said to have passed the test, and have some measure of intelligence.

The questions must be typewritten so as not to rely on the machine's grasp of spoken language. The results of the test also don't rely on the machine producing the correct answer to the question, just a coherent, human-like answer.

Building on these work computer scientists engineered a reverse Turing Test so that a computer may recognize when it is interacting with a human, rather than another computer. CAPTCHA, the skewed image of an alphanumeric code you have to type into a website before doing something like buying concert tickets or leaving a comment on a blog post, protect the website from spam or other misuse from automated systems.

In 1952 Alan set his sights on a different kind of science. Where he had been mostly involved in mathematics and computer science thus far in his adult life, he now became interested in chemistry as it related to animal biology. He specifically wanted to look at morphogenesis, the process by which animals develop spots and patterns on their skin, scaled, or fur, or how plants develop certain patterns on their leaves. Turing published a paper called The Chemical Basis of Morphogenesis.

In this paper Turing proposed a process called intercellular reaction-diffusion. Identical cells are either inhibited or excited by various chemicals moving through the system. The cells then either present a certain characteristic, or suppress it. This process produces a pattern like a zebra's stripes, or a leopard's spots. These ideas remained theoretical, as Alan was more a computer scientists than a biologist. However, his ideas are still being looked into today as the possible basis for certain patterns on animals.

Later Life and Convictions

In December of 1951 Alan met and began a relationship with a 19 year old man named Arnold Murray. Alan suspected Arnold of stealing money from him after they spent the night together at Alan's house. Arnold denied stealing from him, but did admit he was in some debt, prompting Alan to lend him money on several occasions.

On January 23rd 1952, Alan came home to find his house had been burgled. Nothing of much value had been taken, though a pocketwatch that was a family heirloom was missing. Regardless of the monetary value of what was stolen, the robbery was still a disturbing occurrence. In early February,

Arnold admitted to Alan that his friend, Harry, was the one who robbed him.

Alan went to the police to report the identity of the robber to find that Harry had already been apprehended on unrelated charges. While reporting what he knew, Alan was questioned about his relationship with Murray. He admitted to police their relationship was of a sexual nature. Alan and Arnold were both arrested, and charged with "gross indecency" under Section 11 of the Criminal Law Amendment Act 1885.

This act, also known as the Labouchere Amendment, made homosexual acts, in cases where sodomy could not be proven, illegal. The act was replaced just 15 years later with the Sexual Offences Act 1967 which decriminalized homosexual acts between two consenting males, in private, so long as both individuals were aged 21 or older.

The initial committal proceedings were on February 27th, 1952. Turing's solicitor did not argue for his innocence as, under the laws of the time, Alan was technically guilty. His council and his family advised him to plead guilty. In the trial on March 31st, Alan pled guilty to the charges he faced. He was given the option between imprisonment, or probation and a hormone treatment. He chose the latter.

Arnold Murray was let off with a conditional discharge; essentially a probation period where he would not be charged for the crime at hand, on the condition that he was not arrested for any similar crimes in a stated period.

The hormone treatment consisted of a year of stilboestrol injections. This substance was a synthetic oestrogen that was meant to lower Turing's sex drive. The end result was essentially a chemical castration. The injections rendered him sterile, and allegedly caused a condition known as gynaecomastia, an increase in the glandular tissue around the nipples due to a hormone imbalance, giving the appearance of female breasts.

Alan also had his security clearances removed because of the conviction. As a result, he was no longer able to work on his cryptographic consultancy for the

Government Communications
Headquarters.

Death Theories

On June 8th, 1954 Alan Turing's housekeeper found him dead in his bedroom. A half-eaten apple lay by his bedside. A subsequent inquest determined the cause of his death was suicide by cyanide poisoning. Turing had allegedly laced the apple with the chemical, and ate it before bed. He, like his father, was cremated at Woking Crematorium, and his ashes were scattered on the grounds.

Several Turing biographers (including the director of the hit film The Imitation Game, based on Turing's life) believe his death was, in fact, a suicide, based on Alan's obsession with Snow White and the Seven Dwarfs. Turing was apparently enchanted by the film and particularly interested in the scene where the Evil Queen dips the apple into poison before feeding it to Snow White. They believe his suicide was a reenactment of this scene.

This scenario feeds into the narrative that has grown up around Turing since his death. He has been painted as an oppressed, hounded individual who became so depressed by his conviction and subsequent punishment that he took his own life. However, many do not believe this version of Turing existed in reality.

Jack Copeland, a professor of Philosophy at the University of Canterbury, and an expert on Turing's life, has laid out many pieces of evidence pointing to Turing's death being an accident.

Copeland claims it wasn't unusual for Alan to take an apple to bed, and that he often didn't finish it. The mere existence of the half-eaten fruit on the scene is far from definitive proof of a suicide. There is also the fairly ridiculous fact that the apple was never even tested for cyanide. The idea that Alan killed himself with a poison-laced apple was just an assumption made by investigators. The apple could have accidentally come into contact with the substance, or could have been completely free of cyanide altogether.

Deniers of the suicide theory also point out the fact that, not only did Alan not leave a suicide note of any kind, he actually had reminders on his desk of what needed to be completed in the following week, a list that would obviously be unnecessary if Alan was planning on taking his life.

Then there is the odd timing of his death. Those who think he committed suicide say he was so depressed by his conviction and punishment that he became suicidal. However, Alan went through an entire year of hormone therapy, and, at the time of his death, yet another year had passed since the therapy had ended. He was two years removed from the worst of the scandal, and his punishment was over.

In that two years he was said to have borne his punishment with "amused fortitude".

Friends and family said he showed no signs that he was particularly distressed by the sentencing. Copeland has said, "In a way, we have, in modern times been recreating the narrative of Turing's life, and we have recreated him as an unhappy young man who committed suicide. But the evidence is not there".

Indeed, friends say he was in his usual high spirits the week before his death, throwing a tea party for his young neighbour, and staying the weekend at his close friend Robin Gandy's house. Gandy said he, "seemed, if anything, happier than usual."

It is not unusual for those who have decided on suicide to suddenly brighten before their death; feeling a weight lifted from their shoulders, as they know their suffering will soon be over. However, this doesn't necessarily seem to be the case with Turing. It seems he never experienced the sadness or despondency that usually precedes that sudden upswing. By all accounts, Alan was as upbeat as ever before his death.

That being said, Alan was always an eccentric personality with fairly odd mannerisms. A friend, Geoffrey Jefferson, described Alan's behavior as, "so unversed in worldly ways, so childlike, so non-conformist, so very absent-minded... a sort of scientific Shelley." He always seemed slightly disconnected from reality.

Alan was said to lock his tea mug to the radiator when he was finished work for the day; he would wear a gas mask to work when his allergies were acting up; he sometimes wore a necktie to keep his trousers up, instead of an actual belt; and apparently more than once he would show up to work in his pajamas. A colleague even said Alan once came to work with an alarm clock tied around his waist. He was generally disheveled and always quite absent-minded about his appearance and how he came across to others.

Some close to Alan seemed to notice that the stress of the war and his important work had somewhat gotten to him. Though he was always eccentric, he seemed somewhat manic nearing the end of the war.

There was a story circulating that Alan had withdrawn all his money from his bank accounts and buried the cash on the grounds at Bletchley so he would have access to his money in the event of a German invasion. This story paints the picture of a paranoid, distressed individual who was unnecessarily worried about the future.

His brother, John, however, saw nothing particularly odd about Alan's behavior. Of the story of Alan burying all his money, John said, "In fact, he did nothing of the kind. He had decided that if there were a German invasion, banking accounts would be useless, so he bought some silver ingots for use on the black market. These he trundled in an ancient perambulator and buried in a field (not at Bletchley), where he made a sketch map of their position so he could find them after the war. After the war, he enlisted the help of his friend, Donald Michie, to dig up these ingots - using, typically, a homemade metal detector - but the heavy ingots were by now well on their way to Australia and were never seen again."

John saw this as Alan taking some precautions against a possible German invasion; securing his future. That is not to say that John believed his brother was at all in his right mind, or that his death was an accident. John did believe Alan had committed suicide, though, mostly at his mother's urging, he attempted to find any evidence that it was an accident.

Whether or not Alan became unhinged after the war is difficult to prove. Some saw him in high spirits and never saw him any other way; some thought his behavior was even odder than usual; and some just thought Alan was being authentically Alan. There is no way to know for certain at this point whether or not he was acting particularly unusually, or what his state of mind really was.

Upon investigation of Alan's body, the coroner said, "I am forced to the conclusion that this was a deliberate act. In a man of his type, one never knows what his mental processes are going to do next." He claimed that "the balance of [Turing's] mind was disturbed" at the time of his death, which led him to suicide. It seems the coroner was aware of Alan's trademark eccentricities. However, it is unscientific to assume Alan's death was a suicide just because he occasionally acted oddly and could potentially have wanted to kill himself. Ultimately there is no way the coroner could have known Alan's particular mental state at the time of his death, leading many to question the man's conclusions.

Andrew Hodges, Turing's biographer sums up the confusion around Alan's death beautifully in his book Alan Turing: The Enigma. Hodges writes, "Alan Turing's death came as a shock to those who knew him. It fell into no clear sequence of events. Nothing was explicit - there was no warning, no note of explanation. It seemed an isolated act of self-annihilation...There was no simple connection in the minds of those who had seen him in the previous two years. On the contrary, his reaction had been so different from the wilting, disgraced, fearful, hopeless figure expected by fiction and drama, that those who had seen it could hardly believe that he was dead."

A study of Alan's physical state at the time of his death does not necessarily make the picture any clearer. Looking at the autopsy report, Copeland notes that the distribution of cyanide in Turing's organs was more consistent with inhalation than with ingestion. This would make sense, as Alan had a fairly small, poorly-ventilated laboratory in his house. At the time of his death he was working on electroplating spoons with gold, a process which requires potassium cyanide. Turing could easily have inhaled cyanide fumes and been slowly poisoned to death in his sleep that night.

Alan's marked disinterest in safety procedures also points to an accidental poisoning. Turing seemed to be the very picture of a mad scientist. He had hooked wires from his electrolysis experiments up to the light fixtures of his house and had apparently been so careless with electricity in the past that he had given himself severe electric shocks. He also tended to taste chemicals to figure out what they were.

Though an extremely intellectual person, Alan was known all his life for his absent-mindedness. His mother believed for the rest of her life that her son's death was an accident borne from his characteristic carelessness. Some believe that it was, indeed, cyanide inhalation that caused his death, but that Alan poisoned himself on purpose and made it look accidental in order to protect his mother from the idea that he would take his own life.

This last theory does not line up with what was revealed after his death about Alan's feelings toward his mother. John Turing visited Alan's psychiatrist, Franz Greenbaum, to attempt to glean from him what his brother's mental state was leading up to his death. The psychiatrist gave John two journals of Alan's wherein he had written pages and pages of notes on how he hated his mother. John kept this information from their mother. She never knew of her son's feelings about her, and continued to search for evidence of an accidental poisoning. In light of this information it is rather unlikely that Alan staged a suicide to look like an accident in order to protect his mother, or anyone else for that matter.

One thing that could possibly point to his death as a suicide is the fact that Alan rewrote his will a short time before he died. On February 11th, 1954 he updated his will, making his friend Nick Furbank the executor. Alan left money to his brother's family, his housekeeper, three friends, and his mother. John believed the money that went to his mother was more out of a sense of familial duty, rather than because he actually wanted to give her money.

It is not necessarily unusual for such a young man to have a will though, as many people expect to outlive their parents, it could be considered strange that Alan included his mother in it at all. This could be evidence that Alan considered suicide. However, the will also specified that Alan's housekeeper was to get an additional £10 for each year she had worked for him after the end of 1953. This provision obviously makes no sense if Alan was actually planning to end his life soon after writing the will.

Another theory about Turing's death is much more sinister. Author Roger Bristow claims Alan was murdered by the FBI, who then made it look like a suicide. Bristow says that Turing was working on secret cryptanalysis projects for the Americans before his death. Dubbed Operation Verona, the project was allegedly centered on deciphering radio signals to locate Russian agents undercover in America. Bristow alleges that Turing must have found out sensitive secrets that would embarrass or otherwise harm the government.

The author points out that there is a note on the post mortem report by the pathologist who examined Turing that read, "Death appears to be due to violence." He seems to think that the final verdict on Turing's death is that it was caused by extreme bodily harm, and that the cyanide found in his body was either administered to him during the murder, or was incidental; a side-effect of Turing's careless lab practices. Bristow said, "I don't know if someone who has taken cyanide is able to beat themselves up, but it seems totally incompatible with the line used previously."

There are others who speculate that Alan was murdered simply because he knew too much about cryptanalysis, and the British government's code cracking procedures. He did have high level knowledge of government secrets, and he had lost his security clearance as he was technically a convicted criminal. Some think this put him in a vulnerable position and he was taken out before he could leak government secrets, or be made by enemies to reveal them.

It has also been suggested that he was murdered because his homosexuality somehow put him at risk for blackmail schemes. However, it is well documented that Alan did not hide is orientation, and he had already been convicted of gross indecency, so there was not really much of a threat to him.

The fact that the apple was never tested for cyanide, but the inquest claimed that it was the cause of his death is evidence of either gross incompetence in the police department, or of some sort of cover up. In 2013, human rights activist Peter Tatchell wrote to the British Prime Minister asking for a new inquest into Alan Turing's death. Though he admits there is "no evidence that Turing was murdered by state agents", he does point out that "the fact that this possibility has never been investigated is a major failing."

However he died, the inquest into Alan Turing's death was nowhere near as thorough as it should have been. There are far too many completely plausible and totally uninvestigated possibilities as to how he may have died to ever know for sure whether it was suicide, an accident, or murder.

It is obvious, though, that Alan was treated harshly and unfairly by many throughout his life for both his strange eccentricities, and his open homosexuality. Though he seemed to many to be unfazed by his persecution, his brother firmly believed it was the treatment Alan received from others that led him to take his own life. John Turing said of his brother,"He was a complex man and much loved by many. Had he been better understood when he was young - and if I, among others, had treated him with more consideration - he might be alive today."

Pardoning

In August of 2009, programmer and Oxford alum John Graham-Cumming started a petition that urged the British government to apologize for prosecuting Turing as gay. It received over 30,000 signatures and got the attention of government officials.

In a statement on September 10th 2009, British Prime Minister Gordon Brown said, "Thousands of people have come together to demand justice for Alan Turing and recognition of the appalling way he was treated. While Turing was dealt with under the law of the time and we can't put the clock back, his treatment was of course utterly unfair and I am pleased to have the chance to say how deeply sorry I and we all are for what happened to him ... So on behalf of the British government, and all those who live freely thanks to Alan's work I am very proud to say: we're sorry, you deserved so much better."

An apology, however, is not the same as a pardon. It acknowledges a misdoing, but does not fix it. Turing's conviction was still technically on the books and he was still a criminal in the eyes of the law.

John Leech, the Member of Parliament for Manchester-Withington submitted several bills to parliament that would overturn Turing's conviction. He claimed that, due to Alan's position as a British hero who helped win the war, and current society's completely different view on homosexuality, it was "ultimately just embarrassing" that his conviction still stood.

An e-petition for a full pardoning of Alan Turing, circulated by William Jones in 2011, garnered over 37,000 signatures. Jones and Leech campaigned together to bring attention to their mission. They met opposition from some law officials, including Lord McNally who claimed that, though Turing's persecution was "both cruel and absurd", he was technically rightfully convicted under the laws of the time.

Homosexual sexual acts were illegal, and Turing did plead guilty to the charges. There have been many laws in history that have been overturned, but that does not mean that certain acts were never illegal, or that the government should undertake the daunting and ultimately fruitless task of posthumously pardoning everyone who ever did something illegal that is no longer illegal.

Some felt that pardoning just one person because of his celebrity would be unfair to the many ordinary men who were also cruelly persecuted under the same laws. Others believed the pardoning of Alan Turing would either be a symbolic pardoning of all other men affected, or be the first step in actually officially pardoning all the others.

On July 26th, 2012 a bill was introduced in the House of Lords for a pardon of Turing under Section 11 of the Criminal Law Amendment Act. The bill had massive support from the scientific community. Stephen Hawking wrote in The Daily Telegraph an open letter to Prime Minister David Cameron urging him to act on the pardon.

The bill passed on its third reading in October 2012, and on December 24th, 2013 Queen Elizabeth II signed the official pardon of Alan Turing.

As it turned out Turing's pardon was the first step in the efforts to pardon others who were likewise convicted. In September 2016 a law, nicknamed the Alan Turing Law, was proposed that would retroactively pardon men convicted under indecency laws for acts related to homosexuality in England and Wales. The law that came into effect in 2017, posthumously pardoned 50,000 men, including Oscar Wilde, and gives the option for 15,000 still-living men to apply for an official pardon.

Conclusion

Hugh Alexander, Alan's colleague at Bletchley Park said of Alan, "There should be no question in anyone's mind that Turing's work was the biggest factor in Hut 8's success. In the early days, he was the only cryptographer who thought the problem worth tackling and not only was he primarily responsible for the main theoretical work within the Hut, but he also shared with Welchman and Keen the chief credit for the invention of the bombe.

It is always difficult to say that anyone is 'absolutely indispensable', but if anyone was indispensable to Hut 8, it was Turing. The pioneer's work always tends to be forgotten when experience and routine later make everything seem easy and many of us in Hut 8 felt that the magnitude of Turing's contribution was never fully realised by the outside world."

Alexander did not know how true that sentiment would end up being. Today we take so many things for granted that were originally completely revolutionary ideas conceived by Alan Turing.

Many say that World War Two would have been won by the Allies eventually, with or without the intelligence gleaned by Turing and his team, but that it was won much faster thanks to the codebreaking at Bletchley Park. However, it is impossible to know whether that really is the case.

The breaking of naval Enigma messages ensured the safety of Allied supply lines in the Atlantic, which brought food, weapons, and other much needed supplies to Allied soldiers. That corridor was also essential for ferrying troops from America to Europe for the D-Day invasions. The war truly may not have gone the same way had Turing not conceived of the Bombe, and broken the naval Enigma.

Without Turing we may not even have the computer as we know it today. Turing was one of the first to conceive of a stored-memory computer that would allow a machine to perform more than one function simply by inputting different programs into it. This is the basis of the computer we all use today, the concept of which has been translated into smartphones, which can perform countless functions in seconds from wherever you happen to be.

Hugh Alexander died in 1974, unaware of the recognition Turing would eventually receive for his genius, and his many contributions to mathematics, computer science, the war effort, and even biology.

Many plaques and statues have been placed at significant places in Turing's life in recognition of his accomplishments, and as apologies for how he was treated. The plaque on one such statue reads, "Father of computer science, mathematician, logician, wartime codebreaker, victim of prejudice".

Turing was named as one of Time Magazine's 100 Most Important People of the 20th Century, and is on BBC's list of the Top 100 Greatest Britons. He has many educational halls, buildings, and laboratories at various universities named after him.

Many people have also immortalized Alan Turing in books and movies; notably, Benedict Cumberbatch in the Oscar winning film The Imitation Game based on Andrew Hodges' in-depth biography Alan Turing: The Enigma.

He could even be said to be a pioneer of gay rights. Though he did not actively campaign for any freedoms for homosexual men, Alan did not hide his orientation, even in a time when homosexuality was illegal. He lived freely as a gay man for most of his life, admitting his sexual preference even to his potential wife, Joan Clarke. He was also the impetus for the retroactive pardoning of thousands of gay men who were convicted under indecency laws at the time.

While some of his colleagues and admirers believed he died not getting the recognition he deserved, Alan Turing is now becoming known as one of the most influential humans of the 20th century. It is not often you can definitively state that the world would be a drastically different place without a certain individual, but with Alan Turing that is exactly the case.

38650173R00148

Printed in Great Britain
by Amazon